Raymond's Checklist

For Traveling in Thailand

Raymond's Checklist
For Traveling in Thailand

By
Raymond Greenlaw

Roxy Publishing, LLC
Savannah, Georgia
United States of America

Copy Editor—Raymond Greenlaw
Cover Design—Robert Greenlaw
Text Design—Raymond Greenlaw
Typesetting—WORD – Garamond 12

Roxy Publishing, LLC
Savannah, Georgia 31419
United States of America

http://drraymondgreenlaw.com

First edition, paperback.

© By Raymond Greenlaw, 2020. All rights reserved.

No portion of this work may be reproduced, stored in a retrieval system, or transmitted in any form or by any means—electronic, mechanical, photocopying, recording, or otherwise—without prior written permission of the publisher.

Travelers assume all of the risks in traveling to any of the destinations in this book. The author doesn't advocate visiting all of these places. Some places may be considered dangerous and life-threatening to visit. The author assumes no liability or responsibility for any traveler. All readers of this book are responsible for their own actions and decisions.

ISBN 978-1-947467-15-6 (paperback)

This Book Belongs To:

Fill in Name

Dedication

To Wongduean "Kig" Bohthong.

Table of Contents

1. This Book Belongs To:..........................v
2. Dedication vi
3. Preface..ix
4. Acknowledgments xi
5. Chapter 1 Introduction and Guidelines..........13
6. Chapter 2 Provinces............................23
7. Chapter 3 Major Cities........................29
8. Chapter 4 Favorite Tourist Destinations........35
9. Chapter 5 National and Marine Parks.............47
10. Chapter 6 Islands................................59
11. Chapter 7 Rivers..................................63
12. Chapter 8 Dams, Reservoirs, and Lakes.........69
13. Chapter 9 Extreme Points..................75
14. Chapter 10 Mountains 79
15. Chapter 11 Scuba Diving Sites 83
16. Chapter 12 Totals 89
17. Chapter 13 Rankings...........................91
18. Chapter 14 Raymond's Thailand Travels 95
19. Chapter 15 Conclusions 99
20. References... 101
21. About the Author............................. 102
22. Other Books by Raymond Greenlaw........... 103
23. Appendix A: Compact Version..........................1

Preface

I'm putting together "Raymond's Checklists" in a series of book. This book follows *Raymond's Checklist for Traveling in the USA*. Most visitors to Thailand see very little of the country, and they don't really know what they're missing. This checklist contains many of Thailand's great destinations that are more or less accessible to the average person. Many Thais haven't been to or even heard of a lot of places mentioned in this book!

My intention is that if someone has been to all of the places on my list, then surely everyone can agree the person is well-traveled in Thailand. As I thought more about creating my list, it became clear that the task wasn't that easy. I would have to make choices about what to include and what to exclude. I also wanted my list to reflect as wide a coverage of the Thailand as possible. The list as presented here reflects the checklist I want to have so I can see places that I'm missing and record where I've been. In short, the list is motivating me to travel more in Thailand.

This book is designed so that a reader can easily keep track of where they've been in Thailand by simply checking boxes. A ranking system is included as a way to see how much of Thailand a traveler has visited according to my list. I used population, size, length, or distribution of locations as metrics. I believe that most readers will feel this list includes many important destinations in Thailand. It may even contain a few places that the best-traveled people in Thailand haven't been to yet.

If the reader feels that I've missed a particularly important destination, by all means, let me know. If you notice a typo, an error, name change, additional national park, and so on, I would like to know so that I can make a correction. I realize that the book may be of limited use to Thais who don't read phonetic Thai, and I hope that one day it can be translated into the Thai language.

I hope that readers will enjoy as much as I do checking off both old and new destinations, learning about new places, and seeing where they stand in their Thailand travels.

Enjoy!

Raymond Greenlaw
December 9, 2020

Acknowledgments

A special thanks to Wongduean "Kig" Bohthong for her endless support and encouragement, and for often stepping out of her comfort zone to be with me.

Sincere thanks to reviewers and to those who provided me with constructive comments on earlier drafts of this work. Your suggestions have helped me to improve this book. I'm indebted to you. Many others have contributed to this project in helping to select the categories for my sub-checklists. A sincere thanks to everyone involved.

Chapter 1
Introduction and Guidelines

(The reader who wants to start immediately checking boxes may skip to Chapter 2.)

Thailand is just over 500,000 square kilometers in area. Few people can wrap their heads around this size. Thailand is a bit smaller than Yemen and a bit larger than Spain. Thailand is a bit smaller than Texas and a bit larger than Montana. Thailand is almost exactly double the size of the United Kingdom. Although only the 50th largest country in the world, Thailand has a population of almost 70,000,000 that ranks it 20th in the world. The population falls just below that of Iran and just above that of the United Kingdom.

At any given time, there are probably about 4,000,000 foreigners living in Thailand and almost half of these come from adjacent countries. There's probably another 400,000 tourists in Thailand at any given time. Most of these tourists arrive in the capital city of Bangkok. They visit the Bangkok area and perhaps go to Pattaya. More adventurous tourists will go to Phuket in the south and perhaps Chiang Mai in the north. Others may also make it to Ayutthaya, Sukhothai, and Chiang Rai. A typical Thai may only travel within their province, take an occasional vacation to an adjacent province, or go to one of the same destinations as the average tourist.

How much of Thailand have such people seen? How much of the "real" Thailand have they seen? My list will help quantify both the quantity and quality of travel of people to Thailand. After careful consideration, research, and solicitation of input from a wide range of travelers, and after incorporating reviewers' suggestions, I came up with my checklist, Raymond's Checklist, to quantify how much travel someone has done in Thailand. The list includes provinces, major cities, and a variety of other items.

The checklist also includes favorite tourist destinations, national and marine parks, islands, rivers, dams, reservoirs, lakes, extreme points, mountains, and scuba diving/snorkeling sites. Naturally, some subjectivity was involved in choosing my checklist's categories. And, of course, I had to cut things off somewhere or the list would have become too unwieldy.

I tried to choose my categories wisely after consulting with experts and filtering their responses. Thailand is a dynamic country. For example, its newest province Bueng Kan came into being only in 2011. In terms of my list, I had to cut categories themselves off at some level of granularity. For example, it isn't practical to break provinces into amphoe (districts), as the list would become too cumbersome and many travelers wouldn't remember exactly which amphoes they'd been to within a given province.

With the concept of 'major cities,' I'm able to distinguish travelers who have achieved a significant geographical coverage of a province's important cities from those who have merely visited a province briefly or only been to its capital city. I've also been careful throughout to choose sights of particular interest to both farangs (foreigners) and Thais. There are some sights listed that Thais wouldn't normally go to and others that farangs wouldn't normally visit. The list contains a great diversity of places.

For the category of national parks, I provide a complete listing. My list is as up-to-date as I can get it, as a number of new parks are being added. For other categories I needed to make choices. It wasn't practical to include a comprehensive list of all the islands of Thailand, as there are 1,430. I needed to pick and choose carefully while trying to employ objective criteria in my selections. I believe most will agree that my list strikes a good balance among being detailed enough, providing good geographical coverage, incorporating important historical locations, and including beautiful well-known places, while not being completely exhaustive. Of course, some people would build a slightly different list.

In constructing my overall list, I always favored a geographical distribution of places. I tried to treat each province fairly. To achieve the desired geographical distribution, in my selections I sometimes deviated from strict adherence to an objective metric such as largest, longest, most populous, and so on. In some cases I included a location that was made famous by an important historical event.

I tried to avoid double listing a location and minimize being able to double count. But, in some case by traveling to one particularly important popular location, you'll be able to check off several boxes at once, for example, in the capital area. Other places that would naturally belong in two or more distinct categories are listed only in one of them. You might feel, for example, that Phu Ruea should be listed under Loei's major cities, but instead it's listed under national parks.

I should point out that spellings in the English alphabet of Thai locations will vary from source-to-source. Sometimes you'll notice a space between two "words" in a name, and at other times, there won't be a space. A letter 'k' may be sometimes written as 'g' or vice versa, a 't' as 'd,' a 'j' as 'ch,' and so on. There are a number of other problematic letters as well. Thais may need to read a name out loud "in English," so they can recognize the place in the Thai language. For more on these issues, please take a look at my book *Essential Conversational Thai: Learning to Speak Thai Quickly while Traveling in Thailand*.

I believe this list is one of the most comprehensive of its nature about traveling in Thailand. If someone has visited all the places on this list, I think everyone will agree that they're an extremely accomplished traveler in Thailand. We could define the phrase *platinum Thailand traveler* as someone who has visited 70% of the places on my checklist.

In addition to the checklist being designed to gauge how much one has traveled in Thailand, it allows for friendly comparisons/competitions of travelers in relation to other family members or seasoned travelers. The ranking system provided near the end of the book allows one to grade the amount of travel completed in Thailand. The chapter giving the totals for the author's travel allows you to compare your travels to mine. Hopefully, the list will motivate people to get out and see more of Thailand.

If you live in Thailand, traveling more of the country will help you to understand the country, its people, and the issues facing the nation. If you're visiting Thailand from another country, traveling more of Thailand will help you to understand these same issues as a resident, but also allow you to compare and contrast the issues facing Thailand with your own country's issues, and to better understand the role that Thailand plays in Asian politics.

With a larger quantity of travel and more time spent traveling in Thailand, I feel one has a higher quality of understanding and knowledge of Thailand. My checklist therefore aids in helping to measure both the quantity and quality of travel in Thailand. It's a diverse country and only by going around to many different provinces of the country, its major cities, favorite tourist destinations, national and marine parks, islands, rivers, mountains, and so on can you truly appreciate and understand this diversity, and the country's history.

As you travel around Thailand, it quickly becomes obvious that people speak differently, eat different foods, and come from different ethnic groups. In short, the culture is different in the different parts of the country. People in various regions of the country are often stereotyped. For example, people in Issarn are friendly, hardworking, dark skinned, and love to eat spicy food. People from Bangkok are uptight, in a rush to get things done, and are always trying to avoid nasty traffic jams. People in the South are known for speaking fast, being savvy in business, and eating seafood. But, to find out if these stereotypes are true, you need to go visit such places personally because, if you never go, you never truly know.

I've found that in all regions of the country the vast majority of people are friendly. Thailand is known as "the Land of Smiles." Thais want to help a person in need and offer assistance to someone who's taking the time to travel to their area. Of course, as in most places in the world, you must exercise caution when visiting unfamiliar areas of big cities and perhaps remote areas. The rewards of travel are great, but there are risks. So, exercise caution when going into unfamiliar places, especially at night.

Now that I've described the places that the list covers and given some motivation for why I wanted to develop such a checklist, let me describe how the list is to be applied. In fact, there are no hard-and-fast rules as to when it's legitimate to check a box on the list. The reader must decide on that using their own judgment. For example, if a traveler stopped at Suvarnabhumi Airport on a flight to Changi Airport in Singapore and had never previously been to Samut Prakan, should they be able to check the Samut Prakan box? I leave that as a personal choice. Some travelers may feel that they needed to leave the airport and walked around to check the Samut Prakan box, but others may feel that just being in Samut Prakan at all is sufficient. Checking the box is right for one type of traveler, but not for another.

It's best for individuals to come up with their own rules for when it's okay to check a box and then stick to their system. It's also important to complete the list with integrity; after all, the list is to measure one's own travels. So, only check boxes that meet the rules as you decided on.

A few words are in order about the layout of the chapters and how to use the checkboxes and accounting system that I've developed. The categories have been designed for ease of use and repeated use. For example, in an alphabetical listing of the provinces, I provide a checkbox next to each province. Once you've visited the province, check the box next to it. Then at the end of the checklist for provinces, I've provided a system of counting.

As you check off a new province, simply circle the next number on the list of numbers for provinces visited. If a traveler has been to five provinces, the numbers 1, 2, 3, 4, and 5 should have been circled in the list of numbers following the list of provinces. It may help to take a look at that list of numbers now in the next chapter. If the traveler then visits a new province, for example goes to Surin, they should check the box next to Surin and then circle the number 6. This process is simply a way of adding one to the total number of provinces already visited.

This system of accounting should save you from having to go through the list and counting up the total number of provinces visited each time that a new province is visited. From time-to-time, such an overall counting may be useful just to make sure the accounting is correct. When all of the checkboxes have been checked in a given category, all the numbers should have been circled, at which point 100% of the items in that category will have been visited. At the end of each subchecklist, I leave some space for notes. Any relevant travel notes pertaining to the list in that given chapter can be written in that space, for example, "Intend to visit Pai next summer with Kae."

The totals computed in each chapter will be carried forward to the "totals" chapter. There you can compute an overall value of how many places you've traveled to in Thailand. In the "rankings" chapter, this number will be interpreted, and a ranking corresponding to that amount of travel is given. Different rankings are given for residents and nonresidents.

In each succeeding chapter, I present the sub-checklists for a given category of places. These are alphabetized to make it easier to search them. Once the categories have all been presented, I provide the "totals" chapter followed by the "rankings" chapter. The final chapter presents conclusions.

For travelers who have a ranking above Roamer+, it may take more than one sitting to complete the checklist initially. I suggest that you complete a category or two per day. Undoubtedly, some places will be missed on this first pass, but over time, as you get used to maintaining the checklist, I believe that most places that you've visited can be remembered. If not, it's always possible to go back!

Finally, in Appendix A, I present a more compact form of the list. For those who don't want to carry an extra book while on the road, you can simply bring along these pages or an electronic version of the list. In the eBook version of this work, I provide essentially just that checklist. Places can be checked off easily as you go.

Chapter 2
Provinces

A goal for some travelers is to visit all of the provinces. I begin by listing these places. Check off the places that you've visited and then total them up at the end of the list. This list contains 77 items.

1. ❑ Amnat Charoen
2. ❑ Ang Thong
3. ❑ Bangkok
4. ❑ Bueng Kan
5. ❑ Buriram
6. ❑ Chachoengsao
7. ❑ Chai Nat
8. ❑ Chaiyaphum
9. ❑ Chanthaburi
10. ❑ Chiang Mai
11. ❑ Chiang Rai

12. ❑ Chonburi
13. ❑ Chumphon
14. ❑ Kalasin
15. ❑ Kamphaeng Phet
16. ❑ Kanchanaburi
17. ❑ Khon Kaen
18. ❑ Krabi
19. ❑ Lampang
20. ❑ Lamphun
21. ❑ Loei
22. ❑ Lopburi
23. ❑ Mae Hong Son
24. ❑ Maha Sarakham
25. ❑ Mukdahan
26. ❑ Nakhon Nayok
27. ❑ Nakhon Pathom
28. ❑ Nakhon Phanom
29. ❑ Nakhon Ratchasima
30. ❑ Nakhon Sawan
31. ❑ Nakhon Si Thammarat
32. ❑ Nan
33. ❑ Narathiwat
34. ❑ Nong Bua Lamphu
35. ❑ Nong Khai
36. ❑ Nonthaburi
37. ❑ Pathum Thani
38. ❑ Pattani
39. ❑ Phang Nga
40. ❑ Phatthalung

41. ❏ Phayao
42. ❏ Phetchabun
43. ❏ Phetchaburi
44. ❏ Phichit
45. ❏ Phitsanulok
46. ❏ Phra Nakhon Si Ayutthaya
47. ❏ Phrae
48. ❏ Phuket
49. ❏ Prachinburi
50. ❏ Prachuap Khiri Khan
51. ❏ Ranong
52. ❏ Ratchaburi
53. ❏ Rayong
54. ❏ Roi Et
55. ❏ Sa Kaeo
56. ❏ Sakon Nakhon
57. ❏ Samut Prakan
58. ❏ Samut Sakhon
59. ❏ Samut Songkhram
60. ❏ Saraburi
61. ❏ Satun
62. ❏ Sing Buri
63. ❏ Sisaket
64. ❏ Songkhla
65. ❏ Sukhothai
66. ❏ Suphan Buri
67. ❏ Surat Thani
68. ❏ Surin
69. ❏ Tak

70. ❑ Trang
71. ❑ Trat
72. ❑ Ubon Ratchathani
73. ❑ Udon Thani
74. ❑ Uthai Thani
75. ❑ Uttaradit
76. ❑ Yala
77. ❑ Yasothon

Initially, circle the total number of provinces that you've visited in the list of numbers presented below. As you check off another province from the preceding list, circle the next number on the following list. When you come back to check a new province off the list of provinces, return to the numbers page to circle the next number. And, this counting process will be carried out for each category on my list.

From time-to-time, it may be helpful to count the total number of provinces checked and verify that the correct number has been circled. For example, if 20 provinces have been visited all numbers up to and including 20 should be circled.

1, 2, 3, 4, 5, 6, 7, 8, 9, 10, 11, 12, 13, 14, 15, 16, 17, 18, 19, 20, 21, 22, 23, 24, 25, 26, 27, 28, 29, 30, 31, 32, 33, 34, 35, 36, 37, 38, 39, 40, 41, 42, 43, 44, 45, 46, 47, 48, 49, 50, 51, 52, 53, 54, 55, 56, 57, 58, 59,

60, 61, 62, 63, 64, 65, 66, 67, 68, 69, 70, 71, 72, 73, 74, 75, 76, 77

As the total is updated carry it forward to the chapter on "totals" and insert the new total in the provinces visited location provided. When 100% complete, check here: ❑ 77/77 completed! Congratulations!

Notes:

_____
_____
_____
_____
_____
_____
_____
_____
_____
_____

Chapter 3
Major Cities

To appreciate a province more fully, it's usually important to have visited its "major" cities. Note that in Thailand, the name of a province is almost always also the name of the province's most important city. The city's name is often prefaced by the word 'mueang' meaning 'town.' I don't write the word 'mueang' in the list, as it's clear when I'm referring to the town.

When I say 'major' cities, not all of my cities are really large. In some cases I've included a popular small town. In others I've chosen a place for its geographical location. And, in still others I've selected a place based on its historical or cultural significance. I've not included all cities that could be considered "major," as some of these are simply highly populated industrial areas.

In my sub-checklist there are some provinces for which I didn't list any cities. In many cases, if you visit a smaller province, you'll automatically visit its important city. Bangkok is listed under provinces. Check off the places that you've visited and then total them up at the end of the list. This list contains 82 items.

1. ❏ Amnat Charoen: Amnat Charoen
2. ❏ Bueng Kan: Bueng Kan
3. ❏ Buriram: Buriram
4. ❏ Chai Nat: Chai Nat
5. ❏ Chaiyaphum: Chaiyaphum
6. ❏ Chanthaburi: Chanthaburi
7. ❏ Chiang Mai: Chiang Mai
8. ❏ Chiang Mai: Fang
9. ❏ Chiang Mai: Omkoi
10. ❏ Chiang Mai: Samoeng
11. ❏ Chiang Rai: Chiang Khong
12. ❏ Chiang Rai: Chiang Rai
13. ❏ Chiang Rai: Mae Chan
14. ❏ Chiang Rai: Mae Sai
15. ❏ Chonburi: Chonburi
16. ❏ Chonburi: Pattaya
17. ❏ Chonburi: Sattahip
18. ❏ Chonburi: Si Racha
19. ❏ Chumphon: Chumphon
20. ❏ Kamphaeng Phet: Kamphaeng Phet
21. ❏ Kanchanaburi: Kanchanaburi

22. ❑ Khon Kaen: Khon Kaen
23. ❑ Lampang: Lampang
24. ❑ Lamphun: Lamphun
25. ❑ Loei: Chiang Khan
26. ❑ Loei: Dan Sai
27. ❑ Loei: Loei
28. ❑ Lopburi: Lopburi
29. ❑ Mae Hong Son: Mae Hong Son
30. ❑ Mae Hong Son: Pai
31. ❑ Mae Hong Son: Mae Sariang
32. ❑ Maha Sarakham: Maha Sarakham
33. ❑ Mukdahan: Mukdahan
34. ❑ Nakhon Pathom: Nakhon Pathom
35. ❑ Nakhon Phanom: Nakhon Phanom
36. ❑ Nakhon Ratchasima: Nakhon Ratchasima
37. ❑ Nakhon Ratchasima: Pak Chong
38. ❑ Nakhon Sawan: Nakhon Sawan
39. ❑ Nakhon Si Thammarat: Nakhon Si Thammarat
40. ❑ Nan: Bo Kluea
41. ❑ Nan: Nan
42. ❑ Narathiwat: Narathiwat
43. ❑ Nong Bua Lamphu: Nong Bua Lamphu
44. ❑ Nong Khai: Nong Khai
45. ❑ Nonthaburi: Nonthaburi
46. ❑ Nonthaburi: Pak Kret
47. ❑ Pathum Thani: Khlong Luang
48. ❑ Pattani: Pattani

49. ❏ Phang Nga: Phang Nga
50. ❏ Phatthalung: Phatthalung
51. ❏ Phayao: Ban Mai
52. ❏ Phetchabun: Phetchabun
53. ❏ Phetchaburi: Phetchaburi
54. ❏ Phichit: Phichit
55. ❏ Phitsanulok: Phitsanulok
56. ❏ Phra Nakhon Si Ayutthaya: Phra Nakhon Si Ayutthaya (also called just Ayutthaya)
57. ❏ Phrae: Phrae
58. ❏ Phuket: Phuket
59. ❏ Prachuap Khiri Khan: Hua Hin
60. ❏ Ranong: Ranong
61. ❏ Ratchaburi: Ratchaburi
62. ❏ Rayong: Rayong
63. ❏ Roi Et: Roi Et
64. ❏ Sakon Nakhon: Sakon Nakhon
65. ❏ Samut Prakan: Samut Prakan
66. ❏ Samut Sakhon: Samut Sakhon
67. ❏ Saraburi: Saraburi
68. ❏ Sisaket: Sisaket
69. ❏ Songkhla: Hat Yai
70. ❏ Songkhla: Songkhla
71. ❏ Sukhothai: Sukhothai
72. ❏ Surat Thani: Surat Thani
73. ❏ Surin: Surin
74. ❏ Tak: Mae Sot
75. ❏ Tak: Tak

76. ❏ Trang: Trang
77. ❏ Trat: Trat
78. ❏ Ubon Ratchathani: Ubon Ratchathani
79. ❏ Udon Thani: Udon Thani
80. ❏ Uttaradit: Uttaradit
81. ❏ Yala: Yala
82. ❏ Yasothon: Yasothon

Initially, circle the total number of major cities that you've visited. As a new city is visited and checked off from the preceding list, circle the next number on the following list:

1, 2, 3, 4, 5, 6, 7, 8, 9, 10, 11, 12, 13, 14, 15, 16, 17, 18, 19, 20, 21, 22, 23, 24, 25, 26, 27, 28, 29, 30, 31, 32, 33, 34, 35, 36, 37, 38, 39, 40, 41, 42, 43, 44, 45, 46, 47, 48, 49, 50, 51, 52, 53, 54, 55, 56, 57, 58, 59, 60, 61, 62, 63, 64, 65, 66, 67, 68, 69, 70, 71, 72, 73, 74, 75, 76, 77, 78, 79, 80, 81, 82

As the total is updated here carry it forward to the chapter on "totals" and insert the new total in the major cities visited location. When 100% complete, check here: ❏ 82/82 completed! Congratulations!

Notes:

Chapter 4
Favorite Tourist Destinations

I've listed some favorite tourist destinations in this chapter. These were selected based on their popularity, historical importance, cultural significance, and beauty. I've chosen to include temples in this section as well, even though these are sacred places of worship. Most tourists to Thailand and many Thais spend a lot of time visiting temples. The Thai word for temple is 'wat.'

Note I've written the names in a way that I think you can easily recognize them, although in some cases the names I've written aren't the official ones, which are often less well-known. Sometimes I give the English name; other times the Thai name is written in phonetics depending on which one is more commonly used. On occasion, I provide both English and Thai names.

I've tried to obtain a good geographical distribution of sites. This decision implies that not all sites are of equal weight. Some provinces have no destinations listed. This omission usually occurs because the important places in these provinces are listed in other categories, for example, national and marine parks.

Check off the places that you've visited and then total them up at the end of the list. This list contains 165 items.

1. ❑ Amnat Charoen: Wat Pho Sila
2. ❑ Amnat Charoen: Wat Saman Rattanaram
3. ❑ Ang Thong: Wat Chanthraram
4. ❑ Bangkok: Canals
5. ❑ Bangkok: Chatuchak Weekend Market
6. ❑ Bangkok: Floating Market
7. ❑ Bangkok: The Grand Palace
8. ❑ Bangkok: Jim Thompson House
9. ❑ Bangkok: Khao San Road
10. ❑ Bangkok: Lumpini Park
11. ❑ Bangkok: Nana Plaza
12. ❑ Bangkok: Patpong
13. ❑ Bangkok: Soi Cowboy
14. ❑ Bangkok: Sukhumvit Road
15. ❑ Bangkok: Wat Arun (Temple of the Dawn)

16. ❑ Bangkok: Wat Pho
17. ❑ Bangkok: Wat Phra Gaew (Temple of the Emerald Buddha)
18. ❑ Bueng Kan: Wat Ahong
19. ❑ Bueng Kan: Wat Phu Tok (Stairways to Heaven)
20. ❑ Buriram: Phanom Rung Historical Park
21. ❑ Chachoengsao: Wat Sothorn
22. ❑ Chai Nat: Wat Phra Borommathat Worawihan
23. ❑ Chaiyaphum: Prang Ku
24. ❑ Chanthaburi: Chanthaboon Old Town
25. ❑ Chiang Mai: Chiang Mai Night Bazaar
26. ❑ Chiang Mai: Mae Fah Luang Art and Cultural Park
27. ❑ Chiang Mai and Chiang Rai: Northern Hill Tribes
28. ❑ Chiang Mai: Queen Sirikit Botanic Garden
29. ❑ Chiang Mai: Royal Park Rajapruek
30. ❑ Chiang Mai: San Kamphaeng Hot Springs
31. ❑ Chiang Mai: Sunday Walking Street Market
32. ❑ Chiang Mai: Wat Chedi Luang
33. ❑ Chiang Mai: Wat Ched Yod
34. ❑ Chiang Mai: Wat Phra That Doi Kham (Temple of the Golden Mountain)

35. ❑ Chiang Mai: Wat Phra That Doi Suthep (Temple of Suthep Mountain)
36. ❑ Chiang Rai: Hall of Opium Museum
37. ❑ Chiang Rai: Phu Chi Fah
38. ❑ Chiang Rai: Wat Rong Khun (White Temple)
39. ❑ Chonburi: Jomtien Beach
40. ❑ Chonburi: Pattaya Floating Market
41. ❑ Chonburi: Pattaya Walking Street
42. ❑ Elephant Sanctuary: Any one of the many will suffice
43. ❑ Kalasin: Phu Faek Forest Park
44. ❑ Kalasin: Sirindhorn Museum and Phu Kum Khao Dinosaur Excavation Site
45. ❑ Kamphaeng Phet: Kamphaeng Phet Historical Park
46. ❑ Kanchanaburi: Bridge on the River Kwai
47. ❑ Kanchanaburi: Death Railway
48. ❑ Kanchanaburi: Hellfire Pass Interpretive Centre and Memorial Walking Trail
49. ❑ Kanchanaburi: Prasat Mueang Sing Historical Park
50. ❑ Kanchanaburi: Thailand-Burma Railway Centre
51. ❑ Kanchanaburi: Three Pagodas Pass
52. ❑ Khon Kaen: Si Wiang Dinosaur Park
53. ❑ Khon Kaen: Wat Nong Wang
54. ❑ Khon Kaen: Wat Thung Setthi

55. ❑ Krabi: Ao Nang
56. ❑ Krabi: Klong Thom Hot Springs
57. ❑ Krabi: Rai Leh Beach
58. ❑ Lampang: Baan Sao Nak
59. ❑ Lampang: Dhanabadee Ceramic Museum
60. ❑ Lampang: Wat Phra Kaeo Don Tao Suchadaram
61. ❑ Lamphun: Wat Phra That Hariphunchai
62. ❑ Lamphun: Wat San Pa Yang Luang
63. ❑ Loei: Erawan Cave
64. ❑ Loei: Wat Pahuaylad Temple
65. ❑ Lopburi: King Narai's Palace
66. ❑ Lopburi: Phra Prang Sam Yod
67. ❑ Lopburi: Wat Phra Si Ratana Maha That
68. ❑ Mae Hong Son: Pai Canyon
69. ❑ Mae Hong Son: Pai Historical Bridge
70. ❑ Mae Hong Son: Tham Lot (Fish Cave)
71. ❑ Maha Sarakham: Wat Phra That Na Dun
72. ❑ Mukdahan: Indochine Market
73. ❑ Mukdahan: Wat Si Mongkhon Tai
74. ❑ Nakhon Nayok: Bamboo Grove Wat Chulaporn Wararam
75. ❑ Nakhon Pathom: Sanam Chandra Palace
76. ❑ Nakhon Pathom: Wat Phra Pathom Chedi
77. ❑ Nakhon Phanom: Paya Sri Satta Nakarat

78. ❑ Nakhon Phanom: Wat Maha That
79. ❑ Nakhon Ratchasima: Giant Banyan Tree (Sai Ngam)
80. ❑ Nakhon Ratchasima: Phimai Historical Park
81. ❑ Nakhon Ratchasima: Thao Suranaree Monument
82. ❑ Nakhon Sawan: Wat Kiriwong
83. ❑ Nakhon Si Thammarat: Wat Chedi (Chicken Temple)
84. ❑ Nan: Nan Walking Street
85. ❑ Nan: Wat Phra That Chae Haeng
86. ❑ Nan: Wat Phra That Khao Noi
87. ❑ Nan: Wat Phumin
88. ❑ Narathiwat: Narathat Beach
89. ❑ Narathiwat: Taloh-manoh Mosque
90. ❑ Nong Bua Lamphu: Somdej Phra Naresuan Maharat Shrine
91. ❑ Nong Bua Lamphu: Wat Thom Klong Pen
92. ❑ Nong Khai: Sala Kaew Ku
93. ❑ Nong Khai: Thai-Lao Friendship Bridge
94. ❑ Nong Khai: Tha Sadet Market
95. ❑ Nong Khai: Wat Pha Tak Sua
96. ❑ Nonthaburi: Wat Sangkhathan
97. ❑ Pathum Thani: The National Museum
98. ❑ Pattani: Krue Se Mosque
99. ❑ Pattani: Pattani Provincial Central Mosque

100. ❏ Pattani: Wat Chang Hai Rat Buranaram
101. ❏ Phang Nga: International Tsunami Museum
102. ❏ Phatthalung: Khao Ok Thalu
103. ❏ Phatthalung: Thale Noi Water Bird Park
104. ❏ Phayao: Phu Langka Forest Park
105. ❏ Phayao: Wat Analayo Thipphayaram
106. ❏ Phetchabun: Wat Pha Sorn Kaew (Temple on a High Glass Cliff)
107. ❏ Phetchaburi: Phra Nakhon Khiri Historical Park
108. ❏ Phichit: Wat Pho Prathap Chang
109. ❏ Phitsanulok: Phra Buddha Chinnarat
110. ❏ Phitsanulok: Phra Si Ratana Temple
111. ❏ Phra Nakhon Si Ayutthaya: Ayutthaya Historical Park
112. ❏ Phra Nakhon Si Ayutthaya: Wat Chaiwatthanaram
113. ❏ Phra Nakhon Si Ayutthaya: Wat Mahathat
114. ❏ Phra Nakhon Si Ayutthaya: Wat Phra Sri Sanphet
115. ❏ Phrae: Khum Chao Luang
116. ❏ Phrae: Wat Phra That Cho Hae
117. ❏ Phuket: Bangla Road
118. ❏ Phuket: Bang Tao Beach
119. ❏ Phuket: Big Buddha
120. ❏ Phuket: Freedom Beach

121. ❏ Phuket: Karon Beach
122. ❏ Phuket: Phang Nga Bay
123. ❏ Phuket: Promthep Cape
124. ❏ Prachinburi: Prachinburi National Museum
125. ❏ Prachuap Khiri Khan: Ao Manao
126. ❏ Prachuap Khiri Khan: Hua Hin Beach
127. ❏ Prachuap Khiri Khan: Wing 5
128. ❏ Ratchaburi: Damnoen Saduak Floating Market
129. ❏ Ratchaburi: Khao Ngoo (Snake) Rock Park
130. ❏ Roi Et: Phalanchai Park
131. ❏ Roi Et: Wat Pha Nam Yoi
132. ❏ Sa Kaeo: Phrasat Khao Noi
133. ❏ Sakon Nakhon: Wat Phra That Choeng Chum Worawihan Temple
134. ❏ Samut Prakan: Ancient City
135. ❏ Samut Prakan: Erawan Museum
136. ❏ Samut Prakan: Wat Asokaram
137. ❏ Samut Sakhon: Wat Ketmadi Si Waram
138. ❏ Samut Songkhram: Amphawa Floating Market
139. ❏ Samut Songkhram: Maekhlong Railway Market
140. ❏ Saraburi: Wat Pasawangboon
141. ❏ Sing Buri: Monument of Bang Rachan Heroes

142. ❏ Sisaket: Prasat Hin Wat Sa Kampaeng Yai
143. ❏ Songkhla: Tang Kuan Hill
144. ❏ Sukhothai: Sukhothai Historical Park
145. ❏ Suphan Buri: Wat Pa Lelai Woraviharn
146. ❏ Surat Thani: Surat Thani City Pillar Shrine
147. ❏ Surin: Surin National Museum
148. ❏ Tak: Giant Krabak Tree
149. ❏ Tak: Tee Lor Su Waterfall
150. ❏ Tak: Thailand-Myanmar Friendship Bridge
151. ❏ Tak: Wat Thai Wattanaram
152. ❏ Ubon Ratchathani: Wat Nong Pah Pong
153. ❏ Ubon Ratchathani: Wat Phra That Nong Bua
154. ❏ Udon Thani: National Museum of Ban Chiang
155. ❏ Udon Thani: Nong Prajak Public Park
156. ❏ Udon Thani: Phu Phrabat Historical Park
157. ❏ Uthai Thani: Giant Tree in Baan Rai
158. ❏ Uthai Thani: Wat Tham Khao Wong
159. ❏ Uthai Thani: Wat Tha Sung
160. ❏ Uttaradit: Praya Phichai Dap Hak Memorial
161. ❏ Uttaradit: Sak Yai Forest Park
162. ❏ Uttaradit: Wat Phra Thaen Sila At

163. ❑ Yala: Piyamit Tunnels and Millennium Tree
164. ❑ Yala: Talay Mok Aiyoeweng
165. ❑ Yasothon: Phu Tham Phra

Initially, circle the total number of favorite tourist destinations visited. As you check off a tourist destination from the preceding list, circle the next number on the following list.

1, 2, 3, 4, 5, 6, 7, 8, 9, 10, 11, 12, 13, 14, 15, 16, 17, 18, 19, 20, 21, 22, 23, 24, 25, 26, 27, 28, 29, 30, 31, 32, 33, 34, 35, 36, 37, 38, 39, 40, 41, 42, 43, 44, 45, 46, 47, 48, 49, 50, 51, 52, 53, 54, 55, 56, 57, 58, 59, 60, 61, 62, 63, 64, 65, 66, 67, 68, 69, 70, 71, 72, 73, 74, 75, 76, 77, 78, 79, 80, 81, 82, 83, 84, 85, 86, 87, 88, 89, 90, 91, 92, 93, 94, 95, 96, 97, 98, 99, 100, 101, 102, 103, 104, 105, 106, 107, 108, 109, 110, 111, 112, 113, 114, 115, 116, 117, 118, 119, 120, 121, 122, 123, 124, 125, 126, 127, 128, 129, 130, 131, 132, 133, 134, 135, 136, 137, 138, 139, 140, 141, 142, 143, 144, 145, 146, 147, 148, 149, 150, 151, 152, 153, 154, 155, 156, 157, 158, 159, 160, 161, 162, 163, 164, 165

As the total is updated here carry it forward to the chapter on "totals" and insert the new total in the favorite tourist destinations visited location pro-

vided there. When 100% complete, check here: ❑
165/165 completed! Congratulations!

Notes:

___
___
___
___
___
___
___
___
___
___

Chapter 5
National and Marine Parks

Thailand's national and marine parks are a great source of pride for Thai people. These places are special for their natural beauty, flora, wildlife, and geology, and as such have been designated as places that should be preserved for future generations to enjoy. I've included all confirmed national and marine parks.

There are a large number of additional areas under consideration for national- or marine park status, so this is a dynamic category. Although there are many extraordinarily beautiful provincial parks as well, it didn't make sense to list parks at that granularity in my checklist. I also didn't list the wildlife sanctuaries and forest parks, though these are certainly worth visiting. A few such parks did make the favorite tourist destinations sub-checklist.

The first national park to be established in Thailand was Khao Yai in 1961. The first national marine park was Khao Sam Roi Yot in 1966. Since then many more have been created, and new ones are being added regularly. The national and marine parks have difficulty in preventing illegal farming, poaching, logging, burning, fishing, and encroachment. The park system has been criticized for excessive development of park lands. The corruption level—Thailand falls basically in the middle of all countries in the rankings—in the country means that the wealthy can get private concessions on the land. Those without means have little to lose if they violate park regulations. Hopefully, in the future the parks can receive better protection and be preserved as intended.

Simply check off the places that you've visited and then total them up at the end of the list. This list contains 131 items. I hope to update it over time, as new parks are confirmed.

1. ❑ Buriram and Sa Kaeo: Ta Phraya National Park
2. ❑ Chaiyaphum: Pa Hin Ngam National Park
3. ❑ Chaiyaphum: Phu Laenkha National Park
4. ❑ Chaiyaphum: Sai Thong National Park
5. ❑ Chaiyaphum: Tat Ton National Park
6. ❑ Chanthaburi: Khao Khitchakut National Park

7. ❑ Chanthaburi: Khao Sip Ha Chan National Park
8. ❑ Chanthaburi: Namtok Phlio National Park
9. ❑ Chiang Mai: Doi Inthanon National Park
10. ❑ Chiang Mai: Doi Pha Hom Pok National Park
11. ❑ Chiang Mai: Doi Suthep-Pui National Park
12. ❑ Chiang Mai: Huai Nam Dang National Park
13. ❑ Chiang Mai: Khun Khan National Park
14. ❑ Chiang Mai: Mae Wang National Park
15. ❑ Chiang Mai: Op Luang National Park
16. ❑ Chiang Mai: Pha Daeng National Park
17. ❑ Chiang Mai: Si Lanna National Park
18. ❑ Chiang Rai, Lampang, and Phayao: Doi Luang National Park
19. ❑ Chiang Rai: Khun Chae National Park
20. ❑ Chumphon: Mu Koh Chumphon National Marine Park
21. ❑ Kamphaeng Phet: Khlong Lan National Park
22. ❑ Kamphaeng Phet and Tak: Khlong Wang Chao National Park
23. ❑ Kamphaeng Phet and Nakhon Sawan: Mae Wong National Park
24. ❑ Kanchanaburi: Chaloem Rattanakosin National Park

25. ❑ Kanchanaburi: Erawan National Park
26. ❑ Kanchanaburi: Khao Laem National Park
27. ❑ Kanchanaburi: Khuean Srinagarindra National Park
28. ❑ Kanchanaburi: Lam Khlong Ngu National Park
29. ❑ Kanchanaburi: Sai Yok National Park
30. ❑ Kanchanaburi: Thong Pha Phum National Park
31. ❑ Khon Kaen and Chaiyaphum: Nam Phong National Park
32. ❑ Khon Kaen: Phu Kao-Phu Phan Kham National Park
33. ❑ Khon Kaen and Loei: Phu Pha Man National Park
34. ❑ Khon Kaen: Phu Wiang National Park
35. ❑ Krabi: Hat Noppharat Thara-Mu Koh Phi Phi National Marine Park
36. ❑ Krabi: Khao Phanom Bencha National Marine Park
37. ❑ Krabi: Mu Koh Lanta National Marine Park
38. ❑ Krabi: Than Bok Khorani National Park
39. ❑ Lampang: Chae Son National Park
40. ❑ Lampang and Tak: Mae Wa National Park
41. ❑ Lamphun: Doi Khun Tan National Park

42. ❏ Lamphun, Chiang Mai, and Tak: Mae Ping National Park
43. ❏ Loei: Phu Kradueng National Park
44. ❏ Loei: Phu Ruea National Park
45. ❏ Loei: Phu Suan Sai National Park
46. ❏ Mae Hong Son: Namtok Mae Surin National Park
47. ❏ Mae Hong Son: Salawin National Park
48. ❏ Mae Hong Son: Tham Pla-Namtok Pha Suea National Park
49. ❏ Mukdahan: Phu Pha Thoep National Park
50. ❏ Mukdahan, Ubon Ratchathani, and Yasothon: Phu Sa Dok Bua National Park
51. ❏ Nakhon Phanom: Phu Langka National Park
52. ❏ Nakhon Ratchasima, Nakhon Nayok, Prachinburi, and Saraburi: Khao Yai National Park
53. ❏ Nakhon Si Thammarat: Khao Luang National Park
54. ❏ Nakhon Si Thammarat: Khao Nan National Park
55. ❏ Nakhon Si Thammarat and Surat Thani: Namtok Si Khit National Park
56. ❏ Nakhon Si Thammarat: Namtok Yong National Park
57. ❏ Nan: Doi Phu Kha National Park
58. ❏ Nan: Khun Nan National Park

59. ❑ Nan: Mae Charim National Park
60. ❑ Nan: Si Nan National Park
61. ❑ Narathiwat, Pattani, and Yala: Budo-Su-Ngai Padi National Park
62. ❑ Pattani, Songkhla, and Yala: Namtok Sai Khao National Park
63. ❑ Phang Nga: Ao Phang-Nga National Marine Park
64. ❑ Phang Nga: Khao Lak-Lam Ru National Marine Park
65. ❑ Phang Nga: Khao Lampi-Hat Thai Mueang National Marine Park
66. ❑ Phang Nga: Mu Koh Similan National Marine Park
67. ❑ Phang Nga: Mu Koh Surin National Marine Park
68. ❑ Phang Nga: Si Phang-Nga National Park
69. ❑ Phatthalung: Khao Pu-Khao Ya National Park
70. ❑ Phayao: Doi Phu Nang National Park
71. ❑ Phayao and Chiang Rai: Mae Puem National Park
72. ❑ Phayao and Chiang Rai: Phu Sang National Park
73. ❑ Phetchabun: Khao Kho National Park
74. ❑ Phetchabun: Nam Nao National Park
75. ❑ Phetchabun: Tat Mok National Park

76. ❑ Phetchaburi and Prachuap Khiri Khan: Kaeng Krachan National Park
77. ❑ Phitsanulok: Kaeng Chet Khwae National Park
78. ❑ Phitsanulok: Namtok Chat Trakan National Park
79. ❑ Phitsanulok and Loei: Phu Hin Rong Kla National Park
80. ❑ Phitsanulok and Phetchabun: Thung Salaeng Luang National Park
81. ❑ Phrae: Doi Pha Klong National Park
82. ❑ Phrae: Mae Yom National Park
83. ❑ Phrae and Lampang: Wiang Kosai National Park
84. ❑ Phuket: Sirinat National Marine Park
85. ❑ Prachinburi and Nakhon Ratchasima: Thap Lan National Park
86. ❑ Prachuap Khiri Khan: Hat Wanakon National Marine Park
87. ❑ Prachuap Khiri Khan: Khao Sam Roi Yot National Marine Park
88. ❑ Prachuap Khiri Khan: Kui Buri National Park
89. ❑ Prachuap Khiri Khan: Namtok Huai Yang National Park
90. ❑ Ranong: Laem Son National Marine Park
91. ❑ Ranong: Lam Nam Kra Buri National Marine Park

92. ❏ Ranong: Mu Koh Ranong National Marine Park
93. ❏ Ranong and Chumphon: Namtok Ngao National Park
94. ❏ Ratchaburi: Chaloem Phrakiat Thai Prachan National Park
95. ❏ Rayong and Chanthaburi: Khao Chamao-Khao Wong National Park
96. ❏ Rayong: Khao Laem Ya-Mu Koh Samet National Marine Park
97. ❏ Sa Kaeo and Prachinburi: Pang Sida National Park
98. ❏ Sakon Nakhon and Udon Thani: Phu Pha Lek National Park
99. ❏ Sakon Nakhon and Kalasin: Phu Phan National Park
100. ❏ Sakon Nakhon, Mukdahan, and Nakhon Phanom: Phu Pha Yon National Park
101. ❏ Saraburi: Namtok Sam Lan National Park
102. ❏ Satun and Trang: Mu Koh Phetra National Marine Park
103. ❏ Satun: Tarutao National Marine Park
104. ❏ Satun: Thale Ban National Marine Park
105. ❏ Sisaket and Ubon Ratchathani: Khao Phra Wihan National Park
106. ❏ Songkhla: Khao Nam Khang National Park

107. ❏ Sukhothai: Ramkhamhaeng National Park
108. ❏ Sukhothai: Si Satchanalai National Park
109. ❏ Suphan Buri: Phu Toei National Park
110. ❏ Surat Thani: Kaeng Krung National Park
111. ❏ Surat Thani: Khao Sok National Park
112. ❏ Surat Thani: Khlong Phanom National Park
113. ❏ Surat Thani: Mu Koh Ang Thong National Marine Park
114. ❏ Surat Thani: Tai Rom Yen National Park
115. ❏ Surat Thani: Than Sadet-Koh Pha-Ngan National Park
116. ❏ Tak: Khun Phawo National Park
117. ❏ Tak: Lan Sang National Park
118. ❏ Tak: Mae Moei National Park
119. ❏ Tak: Namtok Pha Charoen National Park
120. ❏ Tak: Taksin Maharat National Park
121. ❏ Trang: Hat Chao Mai National Marine Park
122. ❏ Trat: Mu Koh Chang National Marine Park
123. ❏ Trat: Namtok Khlong Kaeo National Park
124. ❏ Ubon Ratchathani: Kaeng Tana National Park

125. ❏ Ubon Ratchathani: Pha Taem National Park
126. ❏ Ubon Ratchathani: Phu Chong-Na Yoi National Park
127. ❏ Udon Thani: Na Yung-Nam Som National Park
128. ❏ Uttaradit and Phrae: Lam Nam Nan National Park
129. ❏ Uttaradit: Phu Soi Dao National Park
130. ❏ Uttaradit: Ton Sak Yai National Park
131. ❏ Yala: Bang Lang National Park

Initially, circle the total number of national and marine parks visited. As a new national or marine park is visited and checked off from the preceding list, circle the next number on the following list:

1, 2, 3, 4, 5, 6, 7, 8, 9, 10, 11, 12, 13, 14, 15, 16, 17, 18, 19, 20, 21, 22, 23, 24, 25, 26, 27, 28, 29, 30, 31, 32, 33, 34, 35, 36, 37, 38, 39, 40, 41, 42, 43, 44, 45, 46, 47, 48, 49, 50, 51, 52, 53, 54, 55, 56, 57, 58, 59, 60, 61, 62, 63, 64, 65, 66, 67, 68, 69, 70, 71, 72, 73, 74, 75, 76, 77, 78, 79, 80, 81, 82, 83, 84, 85, 86, 87, 88, 89, 90, 91, 92, 93, 94, 95, 96, 97, 98, 99, 100, 101, 102, 103, 104, 105, 106, 107, 108, 109, 110, 111, 112, 113, 114, 115, 116, 117, 118, 119, 120, 121, 122, 123, 124, 125, 126, 127, 128, 129, 130, 131

As the total is updated here carry it forward to the chapter on "totals" and insert the new total in the national and marine parks visited location. When 100% complete, check here: ❑ 131/131 completed! Congratulations!

Notes:

Chapter 6
Islands

Thailand is well-known for its beautiful islands. There are 1,430 islands. I've chosen islands to include here based on their size, location, beauty, accessibility, historical significance, distribution, wildlife, flora, popularity, and importance. Fortunately, many of Thailand's best-known islands are protected in national marine parks. To avoid double counting would seemed contrived in this case. So, if you've been to one of these islands that is in a national marine park, you can check off that park as well. A typical traveler might visit several islands within one park.

Due to overcrowding, damage, efforts to restore, protection of wildlife, or for other reasons, the government may close certain islands. So, please check with the authorities if you're allowed to go on shore at a particular island. Note that sometimes 'island' is spelled 'koh,' 'ko,' or with a 'g.' I consistently use 'koh.'

In the scuba diving sites chapter, a number of other islands are listed. So, you may want to check that list as well. Those are for places you've dived or snorkeled. **Check off the places that you've visited and then total them up at the end of the list.** There are a total of 29 items on this list.

1. ❑ Chonburi: Koh Sichang
2. ❑ Krabi: Koh Kai (Chicken Island)
3. ❑ Krabi: Koh Lanta Yai
4. ❑ Krabi: Koh Phi Phi
5. ❑ Phang Nga: James Bond Island (Koh Khao Phing Kan and Koh Tapu)
6. ❑ Phang Nga: Koh Klang
7. ❑ Phang Nga: Koh Panyi
8. ❑ Phang Nga: Koh Ri
9. ❑ Phang Nga: Koh Surin Tai
10. ❑ Phang Nga: Koh Tapu
11. ❑ Phang Nga: Koh Yao Yai
12. ❑ Ranong: Koh Phayam
13. ❑ Rayong: Koh Samet
14. ❑ Satun: Koh Adang
15. ❑ Satun: Koh Lipe
16. ❑ Satun: Koh Tarutao
17. ❑ Surat Thani: Koh Nang Yuan
18. ❑ Surat Thani: Koh Phaluai
19. ❑ Surat Thani: Koh Pha Ngan

20. ❑ Surat Thani: Koh Samui
21. ❑ Surat Thani: Koh Tao
22. ❑ Trat: Koh Chang
23. ❑ Trat: Koh Kut
24. ❑ Trat: Koh Mak
25. ❑ Trat: Koh Rang
26. ❑ Trang: Koh Kradan
27. ❑ Trang: Koh Libong
28. ❑ Trang: Koh Muk
29. ❑ Trang: Koh Sukon

Note that some double counting will be unavoidable with islands. I'm not going to suggest that someone who only has been to an island belonging to a particular province hasn't been to that province. For example, someone who only has been to Chaweng on Koh Samui will be able to check Surat Thani in the provinces category. It would seem contrived to suggest otherwise.

Initially, circle the total number of islands visited. As a new island is visited and checked off from the preceding list, circle the next number on the following list:

1, 2, 3, 4, 5, 6, 7, 8, 9, 10, 11, 12, 13, 14, 15, 16, 17, 18, 19, 20, 21, 22, 23, 24, 25, 26, 27, 28, 29

As the total is updated here carry it forward to the chapter on "totals" and insert the new total in the islands visited location. When 100% complete, check here: ❑ 29/29 completed! Congratulations!

Notes:

_____
_____
_____
_____
_____
_____
_____
_____
_____
_____

Chapter 7
Rivers

This chapter lists important rivers in the Thailand. I've chosen the rivers based on their length, beauty, historical significance, and importance. In addition, I've chosen them based on their distribution throughout Thailand, trying to make sure that broad regions were covered by at least one river.

Unlike other chapters, here I've listed the destinations in alphabetical order rather than where they fit in a province. The reason is because the rivers often span many provinces. The provinces that a river spans are listed in alphabetical order after the river's name. You should be able to look up rivers easily using alphabetical order.

As always, one must personally decide when it's appropriate to check a box. A swim, long-tail boat trip, or ferry ride in/on the river would certainly suffice, as would travel along a segment of the river. Hiking, cycling, or driving along a portion of the shoreline is also fine. There are 34 checkable items on the list.

1. ❑ Bang Pakong River (Chachoengsao and Prachinburi)
2. ❑ Chanthaburi River (Chanthaburi)
3. ❑ Chao Praya River (Ang Thong, Bangkok, Chainat, Nakhon Sawan, Phra Nakhon Si Ayutthaya, Nonthaburi, Pathum Thani, Samut Prakan, Sing Buri, and Uthai Thani)
4. ❑ Chi River (Chaiyaphum, Kalasin, Khon Kaen, Maha Sarakham, Nakhon Ratchasima, Roi Et, Yasothon, and Ubon Ratchathani)
5. ❑ Hueang River (Loei)
6. ❑ Ing River (Chiang Rai and Phayao)
7. ❑ Khwae Yai River (Kanchanaburi and Tak)
8. ❑ Kok River (Chiang Mai and Chiang Rai)
9. ❑ Li River (Chiang Mai and Lamphun)
10. ❑ Loei River (Loei and Phetchabun)
11. ❑ Lopburi River (Phra Nakhon Si Ayutthaya, and Saraburi)
12. ❑ Mae Khlong River (Kanchanaburi, Ratchaburi, and Samut Songkhram)
13. ❑ Mae Sai River (Chiang Rai)
14. Mekong River (Amnat Charoen, Bueng Kan, Chiang Rai, Loei, Mukdahan, Na-

khon Phahom, Nong Khai, and Ubon Ratchathani) (checkable under extreme points)
15. ❑ Moei River (Mae Hong Son)
16. ❑ Mun River (Buriram, Nakhon Ratchasima, Sisaket, Surin, and Ubon Ratchathani)
17. ❑ Nakon Nayok River (Nakon Nayok and Prachinburi)
18. ❑ Nan River (Nakhon Sawan, Nan, Phichit, Phitsanulok, and Uttaradit)
19. ❑ Noi River (Chainat, Phra Nakhon Si Ayutthaya, and Singburi)
20. ❑ Pak Phanang River (Nakhon Si Thammarat)
21. ❑ Pai River (Mae Hong Son)
22. ❑ Pa Sak River (Loei, Lopburi, Phetchabun, Phra Nakhon Si Ayutthaya, and Saraburi)
23. ❑ Pattani River (Pattani and Yala)
24. ❑ Phachi River (Kanchanaburi and Ratchaburi)
25. ❑ Phetchaburi River (Phetchaburi)
26. ❑ Ping River (Chiang Mai, Kamphaeng Phet, Lamphun, Nakhon Sawan, and Tak)
27. ❑ Ruak River (Chiang Rai)
28. ❑ Sakae Krang River (Chainat, Kamphaeng Phet, and Nakhon Sawan)
29. ❑ Salween River (Mae Hong Son)

30. ❏ Tapi River (Nakhon Si Thammarat)
31. ❏ Tha Chin River (Chainat, Nakhon Pathom, Samut Sakhon, and Suphan Buri)
32. ❏ Trang River (Nakhon Si Thammarat and Trang)
33. ❏ Wang River (Chiang Rai, Lampang, and Tak)
34. ❏ Wa River (Nan)
35. ❏ Yom River (Nakhon Sawan, Phayao, Phichit, Phitsanulok, Phrae, and Sukhothai)

Initially, circle the total number of rivers visited. As a new river is visited and checked off from the preceding list, circle the next number on the following list:

1, 2, 3, 4, 5, 6, 7, 8, 9, 10, 11, 12, 13, 14, 15, 16, 17, 18, 19, 20, 21, 22, 23, 24, 25, 26, 27, 28, 29, 30, 31, 32, 33, 34

As the total is updated here carry it forward to the chapter on "totals" and insert the new total in the rivers visited location. When 100% complete, check here: ❏ 34/34 completed! Congratulations!

Notes:
_____
_____

Chapter 8
Dams, Reservoirs, and Lakes

In this chapter I list important dams, reservoirs, and lakes in Thailand. In order not to be too subjective, I've chosen the dams, reservoirs, and lakes based primarily on their size. Thailand has almost 700 dams, so it wouldn't make sense to list them all. There are many small bodies of water, too. I selected dams, reservoirs, and lakes based on their geographical location as well size in order to obtain a distribution throughout Thailand.

Of course, each dam has a large reservoir associated with it. I didn't list those separately. Many main cities in Thailand have a small lake within a park. I didn't list these either because most people visiting the city would automatically visit the lake. The word 'bueng' means lake.

As always, one must personally decide when it's appropriate to check a box. A swim or boat ride in/on a reservoir or lake would certainly suffice, as would travel along the shore. If you intend to swim, check to make sure that it's allowed and safe. Most bodies of water have many leeches. There are 44 checkable items on the list.

1. ❑ Chai Nat: Chao Phraya Dam
2. ❑ Chaiyaphum: Chulabhorn Dam
3. ❑ Chaiyaphum: Huai Kum Dam
4. ❑ Chiang Mai: Huay Tung Tao Dam
5. ❑ Chiang Mai: Mae Ngat Somboon Chon Dam
6. ❑ Kalasin: Lam Pao Dam
7. ❑ Kanchanaburi: Srinagarind Dam
8. ❑ Kanchanaburi: Tha Thung Na Dam
9. ❑ Kanchanaburi: Vajiralongkorn Dam
10. ❑ Khon Kaen: Ubol Ratana Dam
11. ❑ Loei: Hua Krathing Reservoir
12. ❑ Lopburi: Pa Sak Jolasid Dam
13. ❑ Lopburi: Sub Lek Reservoir
14. ❑ Mae Hong Son: Pang Ung Lake
15. ❑ Maha Sarakham: Khae Loeng Chan Reservoir
16. ❑ Maha Sarakham: Mai Kae Dam
17. ❑ Nakhon Nayok: Khun Dan Prakan Chon Dam

18. ❏ Nakhon Ratchasima: Lam Phra Phloeng Dam
19. ❏ Nakhon Ratchasima: Lam Takhong Dam
20. ❏ Nakhon Sawan: Bueng Boraphet
21. ❏ Nakhon Sawan: Mae Wong Dam
22. ❏ Nakhon Si Thammarat: Khao Phlai Dam
23. ❏ Phayao: Phayao Lake
24. ❏ Phetchaburi: Kaeng Krachan Dam
25. ❏ Phichit: Bueng Si Fai
26. ❏ Phitsanulok: Kwae Noi Bamrung Daen Dam
27. ❏ Phuket: Bang Wad Reservoir
28. ❏ Phrae: Kaeng Suea Ten Dam
29. ❏ Prachinburi: Naruebodindrachinta Reservoir
30. ❏ Prachuap Khiri Khan: Pranburi Dam
31. ❏ Sakon Nakhon: Nam Pung Dam
32. ❏ Sakon Nakhon: Nam Un Dam
33. ❏ Sakon Nakhon: Nong Han Lake
34. ❏ Sisaket: Hua Na Dam
35. ❏ Sisaket: Rasi Salai Dam
36. ❏ Songkhla and Phatthalung: Songkhla Lake (lagoon that has an outlet to the sea)
37. ❏ Sukhothai: Saritphong Dam
38. ❏ Suphan Buri: Krasiao Dam
39. ❏ Surat Thani: Cheow Lan Lake (or Rajjaprabha Dam Reservoir)

40. Tak: Bhumibol Dam (checkable under extreme points)
41. ❑ Ubon Ratchathani: Pak Mun Dam
42. ❑ Ubon Ratchathani: Sirindhorn Dam
43. ❑ Udon Thani: Nong Han Kumphawapi Lake (Red Lotus Lake)
44. ❑ Uttaradit: Sirikit Dam
45. ❑ Yala: Bang Lang Dam

Initially, circle the total number of dams, reservoirs, and lakes visited. As a new place is visited and checked off from the preceding list, circle the next number on the following list:

1, 2, 3, 4, 5, 6, 7, 8, 9, 10, 11, 12, 13, 14, 15, 16, 17, 18, 19, 20, 21, 22, 23, 24, 25, 26, 27, 28, 29, 30, 31, 32, 33, 34, 35, 36, 37, 38, 39, 40, 41, 42, 43, 44

As the total is updated here carry it forward to the chapter on "totals" and insert the new total in the dams, reservoirs, and lakes visited location. When 100% complete, check here: ❑ 44/44 completed! Congratulations!

Notes:

Chapter 9
Extreme Points

In this chapter I list some of the extreme points of Thailand. The directional points are for the mainland, and they don't include islands. Most of these places are easily accessible, but only if one "happens" to be in the area. There are nine checkable items on this list.

1. ❏ Highest Mountain Summit: 2,565 meters, Doi Inthanon, Chiang Mai
2. ❏ Longest River flowing through Thailand: 4,350 kilometers, Mekong River (Amnat Charoen, Bueng Kan, Chiang Rai, Loei, Mukdahan, Nakhon Phahom, Nong Khai, and Ubon Ratchathani)
3. Longest River flowing entirely in Thailand: Some sources say the Chi River is 765 kilometers long and others say it's 1,047 kil-

ometers long; the Mun River is listed as 900 kilometers long. Both rivers are checkable in the rivers chapter.

4. ❏ Tallest Building: 314 meters, King Power Mahanakhon, Bangkok
5. ❏ Highest Dam: 154 meters, Bhumibol Dam, Tak
6. Highest Temperature Ever Recorded: 44.6° C, Mae Hong Son, Mae Hong Son[1] (included elsewhere)
7. Lowest Temperature Ever Recorded: in 1974 −1.4° C, Sakhon Nakhon, Sakhon Nakhon, but may have been lowered recently to −5.0° C at Doi Inthanon Summit, Chiang Mai (included elsewhere)
8. ❏ Biggest Tree in Circumference: 24.2 meters in girth, Koh Yao Noi, Phang Nga
9. ❏ Eastern-Most Point: Pha Taem, Ubon Ratchathani, Laotian border
10. ❏ Western-Most Point: Mae Nam Salawin in Mae Sam Laep, Mae Hong Son, Myanmar border
11. ❏ Northern-Most Point: Mae Sai, Chiang Rai, Myanmar border
12. ❏ Southern-Most Point: Betong, Yala, Malaysian border

---

[1] I was cycling the 600 km long Mae Hong Son loop that day.

Initially, circle the total number of extreme points visited. As a new extreme point is visited and checked off from the preceding list, circle the next number on the following list:

1, 2, 3, 4, 5, 6, 7, 8, 9

As the total is updated here carry it forward to the chapter on "totals" and insert the new total in the extreme points visited location. When 100% complete, check here: ❑ 9/9 completed! Congratulations!

Notes:

Chapter 10
Mountains

There are ten peaks in Thailand over 2,000 meters high. Although there are many other beautiful mountains in the country, I've chosen to list just these ten. You'll find these and many of the others in national parks. As usual, you'll need to decide when it's okay to check a box for a mountain. For many it'll mean that they reached the summit, while for others it'll mean they were on the mountain. Note that some of these summits are difficult to attain, not because of their great heights, but because of their location and the laws involved in going on certain land. A guide may be required by local law.

Exercise good judgement and caution while entering the mountains of Thailand. Don't underestimate the difficulty of the climbs, or the dangers of Thailand's weather, wildlife, insects, and man-made fires. If you don't have a lot of experience, it may be best to hire a guide even if one isn't required. Some areas are closed at certain times of the year due to fires or other issues. It's important not to stray into areas where people are cultivating illegal drugs, hunting, or harvesting items from the forest illegally.

The words 'doi,' 'phu,' and 'khao' all mean mountain. Note that difference sources list different heights for these mountains, so they could be plus or minus a handful of meters either way. There are nine checkable items on this list.

1. Doi Inthanon: 2,565 meters, Chiang Mai (checkable under extreme points)
2. ❑ Doi Pha Hom Pok: Chiang Mai, 2,296 meters
3. ❑ Doi Chiang Dao: Chiang Mai, 2,175 meters
4. ❑ Khao Kacheu Lau: Tak, 2,152 meters
5. ❑ Phu Soi Dao: Uttaradit, 2,120 meters
6. ❑ Phu Khe: Nan, 2,079 meters
7. ❑ Phu Lo: Nan, 2,077 meters
8. ❑ Doi Mae Tho: Chiang Rai, 2,031 meters
9. ❑ Doi Mae Ya: Mae Hong Son, 2,005 meters
10. ❑ Doi Phong Sa Yan: Mae Hong Son, 2,004 meters

Initially, circle the total number of mountains visited. As a new mountain is visited and checked off from the preceding list, circle the next number on the following list:

1, 2, 3, 4, 5, 6, 7, 8, 9

As the total is updated here carry it forward to the chapter on "totals" and insert the new total in the mountains visited location. When 100% complete, check here: ❏ 9/9 completed! Congratulations!

Notes:

_____
_____
_____
_____
_____
_____
_____
_____
_____
_____

Chapter 11
Scuba Diving Sites

Thailand is an underwater paradise. In this chapter I list what are considered to be the best scuba diving sites in Thailand. In order not to be too subjective, I've chosen dive sites based primarily on their popularity and accessibility. A listed "site" may have multiple other named dive sites. I decided not to break things down further than the level presented here. The sites are listed in alphabetical order by name.

For the shallower sites, they can be snorkeled as well. You should feel free to check off the sites that you've snorkeled if you're not a diver. However, don't check off an island simply because you've been to it. To check off items in this list requires getting in the water. To check off islands, visit the chapter specifically about islands. Note that some islands are off limits, and you're not allowed to go ashore.

In numerous cases I've listed an island that has more than one place to dive or is an area where drift diving is common. If you've done any diving or snorkeling there, you can check off that box. Note that not all these sites are of equal difficulty and some require advanced skills.

Never exceed your certification level and abilities. Accidents do happen, and a recompression chamber may be difficult to reach. If you chose to dive with a scuba company in Thailand, you'll need to do your homework to make sure that it's a reputable and safe company. I personally have seen dive boats sinking with passengers on board ...

The word 'hin' means rock or stone. You can search online or visit a scuba shop in Thailand to obtain more information about these sites, to determine if a marine park fee is required to dive there, to learn how to get there, to figure out depths and currents, to determine the best times to dive, and so on. There are 50 items on the list.

1. ❑ Anemone Reef
2. ❑ Anita's Reef (Tsunami Memorial)
3. ❑ Aow Leuk
4. ❑ Boonsung Wreck
5. ❑ Boulder City
6. ❑ Bremen Wreck

7. ❏ Christmas Point
8. ❏ Chumphon Pinnacle
9. ❏ East of Eden
10. ❏ Elephant Head Rock (Hin Pusar)
11. ❏ Hardeep Wreck
12. ❏ Hin Bida
13. ❏ Hin Daeng
14. ❏ Hin Ga Daeng
15. ❏ Hin Kuak Ma
16. ❏ Hin Luk Bat
17. ❏ Hin Muang
18. ❏ Hin Pae
19. ❏ Hin Rap
20. ❏ HTMS Chang
21. ❏ HTMS Khram
22. ❏ HTMS Kut
23. ❏ HTMS Mataphon
24. ❏ HTMS Sattakut
25. ❏ Japanese Garden
26. ❏ King Cruiser Wreck
27. ❏ Koh Bangu
28. ❏ Koh Bida Nai
29. ❏ Koh Bida Nok
30. ❏ Koh Bon
31. ❏ Koh Chi
32. ❏ Koh Dok Mai
33. ❏ Koh Haa
34. ❏ Koh Khai
35. ❏ Koh Khrok

36. ❑ Koh Larn
37. ❑ Koh Nang Yuan
38. ❑ Koh Phi Phi
39. ❑ Koh Sak
40. ❑ Koh Tachai
41. ❑ Racha Noi
42. ❑ Racha Yai
43. ❑ Richelieu Rock
44. ❑ Sail Rock
45. ❑ Shark Fin Reef
46. ❑ Shark Point (Hin Musang)
47. ❑ Southern Rock
48. ❑ Stonehenge (Similan)
49. ❑ Twin Peaks
50. ❑ West of Eden

Initially, circle the total number of scuba dive sites visited either as a diver or snorkeler. As a new scuba dive site is visited and checked off from the preceding list, circle the next number on the following list:

1, 2, 3, 4, 5, 6, 7, 8, 9, 10, 11, 12, 13, 14, 15, 16, 17, 18, 19, 20, 21, 22, 23, 24, 25, 26, 27, 28, 29, 30, 31, 32, 33, 34, 35, 36, 37, 38, 39, 40, 41, 42, 43, 44, 45, 46, 47, 48, 49, 50

As the total is updated here carry it forward to the chapter on "totals" and insert the new total in the scuba dive sites visited location. When 100% complete, check here: ❑ 50/50 completed! Congratulations!

Notes:

Chapter 12
Totals

This chapter is designed to help you compute the overall total of places visited. The subtotals from other chapters should be carried forward to here. Simply copy over from earlier chapters the total number of items visited in each category. I suggest that you use pencil here so that the old totals can be easily erased and the new totals updated.

<u>Category followed by the total number of items visited.</u>

    1. Provinces: _____ / 77

    2. Major Cities: _____ / 82

    3. Favorite Tourist Destinations: _____ / 165

    4. National and Marine Parks: _____ / 131

5. Islands: _____ / 29

6. Rivers: _____ / 34

7. Dams, Reservoirs, and Lakes: _____ / 44

8. Extreme Points: _____ / 9

9. Mountains: _____ / 9

10. Scuba Diving Sites: _____ / 50

Sum up the numbers from the 10 categories and enter (in pencil) that number here: _____ / 630. This number represents the total number of places that you've visited on my checklist. Now please go to the next chapter to obtain a ranking.

Notes:

_____
_____
_____
_____
_____
_____
_____
_____
_____

Chapter 13
Rankings

I've chosen the words Sightseer, Wanderer, Roamer, Pathfinder, Seeker, Traveler, Excursionist, Discoverer, and Explorer, and for the ranking system. A plus symbol (+) is used to indicate the upper portion of a ranking range; a minus symbol (–) is used to denote the beginning portion of a ranking range.

The highest possible ranking is an Explorer and indicates that a person is exceptionally well traveled in Thailand. I don't know if anyone has achieved such a ranking yet. A Sightseer– is the lowest possible ranking and indicates a young traveler or someone who prefers to stay at home.

A non-resident of Thailand can bump his/her ranking up two places. For example, a person who has checked 205 locations on my list (It may help to look ahead a couple of pages.) would be a

Roamer+ if they are a Thailand resident, but a Pathfinder (two places higher) if not a resident of Thailand. For the sake of this checklist, if one was ever a resident of Thailand, they should use the Thailand-resident rankings.

Based on the ranking system, one can make statements such as "I'm a Seeker+ on Raymond's Checklist for traveling in Thailand" or "I hope to move from a Seeker+ to a Traveler– with the big trip that I've planned next summer" or "I would one day love to get to the Discoverer ranking on Raymond's Checklist."

Where one falls in the ranking isn't as important as enjoying traveling, continuing to visit new places, and learning more about Thailand. I believe that it's important to share that experience and knowledge with others who don't have the capability or opportunity to travel. The rankings follow.

<u>Ranking name and the total number of places visited.</u>

Explorer [601..630]

Discoverer+ [576..600]
Discoverer [551..575]
Discoverer– [526..550]

Excursionist+ [501..525]

Excursionist [476..500]
Excursionist− [451..475]

Traveler+ [426..450]
Traveler [401..425]
Traveler− [376..400]

Seeker+ [351..375]
Seeker [326..350]
Seeker− [301..325]

Pathfinder+ [276..300]
Pathfinder [251..275]
Pathfinder− [226..250]

Roamer+ [201..225]
Roamer [176..200]
Roamer− [151..175]

Wanderer+ [126..150]
Wanderer [101..125]
Wanderer− [76..100]

Sightseer+ [51..75]
Sightseer [26..50]
Sightseer− [1..25]

I define anyone who has achieved a ranking of Traveler as *well traveled in Thailand*. I define anyone who has achieved a ranking of Discoverer– or above as a *platinum Thailand traveler*. My hat is off to anyone who reaches the Explorer level!

Notes:

Chapter 14
Raymond's Thailand Travels

In this chapter, as an example, I've listed my totals for each of the categories. I then show how to sum up these subtotals to obtain a ranking.

1. Provinces: 77 / 77

2. Major Cities: 82 / 82

3. Favorite Tourist Destinations: 92 / 165

4. National and Marine Parks: 70 / 131

5. Islands: 8 / 29

6. Rivers: 31 / 34

7. Dams, Reservoirs, and Lakes: 11 / 44

8. Extreme Points: 7 / 9

9. Mountains: 1 / 9

10. Scuba Diving Sites: 28 / 50

Summing up the numbers from the 10 categories leads to 77 + 82 + 92 + 70 + 8 + 31 + 11 + 7 + 1 + 28 = 407. So, I've visited 407/630 or about 65% of the places on my checklist.

Looking back at my results, I see that I still have a lot of favorite tourist destinations, national and marine parks, dams, reservoirs, lakes, mountains, and scuba diving sites to visit. My weakest area is in mountain summits, where I only have visited 20% of the places on my list, including Doi Inthanon. (I only counted mountain summits.) By doing such a simple analysis, you can see where you need to travel in Thailand to expand your horizons … and improve your ranking.

Looking back at the rankings, I see that I'm a Traveler. I'm considered well-traveled in Thailand, according to my ranking system. I would need to visit an additional 19 places to reach the Traveler+ level. I'm setting that as my current short-term goal.

I still have a long way to go to become a platinum Thailand traveler. Seeing where I stand on my list has given me the incentive to do more traveling in Thailand. I now have a better idea of what I'm missing, and I want to see those places. The list has provided me with some new travel goals.

Chapter 15
Conclusions

In mountaineering many lists have been created to inspire climbers. For example, try to bag all peaks in England or all peaks over 14,000 feet (4,242 meters) high in Colorado, and so on. I've many friends who have set as goals checking off all of the boxes on such lists. I hope that my list can serve as a similar source of inspiration for travel in Thailand. I, for one, see that I need to get out and travel more within Thailand.

I've included ten categories on my checklist. There are many other categories that I gave careful consideration to but wasn't able to include. I'm sure that I've missed some wonderful places. By all means go out and visit these places, too. Thailand has much to offer.

In Appendix A, I've included a compact version of the entire list which can be taken on the road rather than carrying a book. I also plan to publish an electronic version of the list, so you can obtain that as well. I believe that such a list would be very good for young children. Both to give them a head start on checking off destinations, but also as a pedagogical tool that touches many different subjects.

In anticipation of future editions of this work, I would appreciate any feedback and corrections. Some of these sub-checklists evolve over time with new places added and others removed. Names can change too so that a particular group can be recognized or a political purpose achieved. I've done my best to make the list as accurate as possible at the time of this writing.

I hope that you are able to reach your travel goals in Thailand. Happy travels!

References

The vast majority of information contained in this book comes from Thai government websites, atlases, maps, and Internet sources, including andamanscuba.com/en, thaiwreckdiver.com, and wikipedia.org (the free encyclopedia). Nearly all of the remainder of the information comes from personal travel, personal communications, and personal knowledge.

A variety of atlases and maps have been used, and the information that I've used from my materials can be found in any atlas or map. In other words no special atlases or maps were used; information about any particular place referred to is easily accessible. On many occasions I've consulted Google™ maps to follow river boundaries, to determine mountain heights, to determine where a destination was located, and to remind me if I'd been there.

Although I tried my best to track down definitive sources, I often encountered contradictions. If you notice any errors, I would appreciate hearing from you and being given the references needed to correct any errors.

About the Author

Raymond "Wall" Greenlaw was born in Providence, Rhode Island, USA in 1961 to Roxy and Bob. Raymond has always enjoyed nature, big trees, lakes, mountains, and the sea. His passion is traveling. He writes about a wide range of topics and is the author of more than 35 books.

Other Books by Raymond Greenlaw

PALMARÈS (also available in electronic form).

The Thai Wife Story JOY (also available in electronic form), Book 1 of *The Thai Wife Series of Novels*.

The Thai Wife Story STAR (also available in electronic form), Book 2 of *The Thai Wife Series of Novels*.

Raymond's Checklist for Traveling in the USA (also available in electronic form), Book 1 of *Raymond's Checklist Series*.

Raymond's Checklist for Traveling in Thailand (also available in electronic form), Book 2 of *Raymond's Checklist Series*.

Raymond's Checklist for Traveling the World (also available in electronic form), Book 3 of *Raymond's Checklist Series*.

Raymond's Checklist for His Personal Bucket List (also available in electronic form), Book 4 of *Raymond's Checklist Series*.

Raymond's Checklist for Gear for a Long Hike (also available in electronic form), Book 5 of *Raymond's Checklist Series.*

Raymond's Checklist Cycling Gear (also available in electronic form), Book 6 of *Raymond's Checklist Series.*

The Hazards of Cycling in Thailand: Guidelines for Tourists (also available in electronic form).

Trapped in Thailand's Cave (also available in electronic form).

The Pacific Crest Trail: Its Fastest Hike, second edition (also available in electronic form).

Bob: My Dad, the Fisherman: A Father and Son's Relationship (also available in electronic form).

(with Saowaluk Rattanaudomsawat) *Essential Conversational Thai: Learn to Speak Thai Quickly, while Traveling in Thailand.*

You'll Never Walk Alone: Love Poems for My Sweetheart (also available in electronic form).

Poems of Raymond Greenlaw, 1986–2005 (also available in electronic form).

The Fastest Hike across Thailand (expected December 2021).

Appendix A: Compact Version

This appendix contains a compact version of the list that can be taken with you while traveling.

Provinces (77)

- ❏ Amnat Charoen
- ❏ Ang Thong
- ❏ Bangkok
- ❏ Bueng Kan
- ❏ Buriram
- ❏ Chachoengsao
- ❏ Chai Nat
- ❏ Chaiyaphum
- ❏ Chanthaburi
- ❏ Chiang Mai
- ❏ Chiang Rai
- ❏ Chonburi
- ❏ Chumphon
- ❏ Kalasin
- ❏ Kamphaeng Phet
- ❏ Kanchanaburi
- ❏ Khon Kaen
- ❏ Krabi
- ❏ Lampang
- ❏ Lamphun
- ❏ Loei
- ❏ Lopburi
- ❏ Mae Hong Son
- ❏ Maha Sarakham
- ❏ Mukdahan
- ❏ Nakhon Nayok
- ❏ Nakhon Pathom
- ❏ Nakhon Phanom
- ❏ Nakhon Ratchasima
- ❏ Nakhon Sawan

- ❏ Nakhon Si Thammarat
- ❏ Nan
- ❏ Narathiwat
- ❏ Nong Bua Lamphu
- ❏ Nong Khai
- ❏ Nonthaburi
- ❏ Pathum Thani
- ❏ Pattani
- ❏ Phang Nga
- ❏ Phatthalung
- ❏ Phayao
- ❏ Phetchabun
- ❏ Phetchaburi
- ❏ Phichit
- ❏ Phitsanulok
- ❏ Phra Nakhon Si Ayutthaya
- ❏ Phrae
- ❏ Phuket
- ❏ Prachinburi
- ❏ Prachuap Khiri Khan
- ❏ Ranong
- ❏ Ratchaburi
- ❏ Rayong
- ❏ Roi Et
- ❏ Sa Kaeo
- ❏ Sakon Nakhon
- ❏ Samut Prakan
- ❏ Samut Sakhon
- ❏ Samut Songkhram
- ❏ Saraburi
- ❏ Satun
- ❏ Sing Buri
- ❏ Sisaket
- ❏ Songkhla
- ❏ Sukhothai
- ❏ Suphan Buri
- ❏ Surat Thani
- ❏ Surin
- ❏ Tak
- ❏ Trang
- ❏ Trat
- ❏ Ubon Ratchathani
- ❏ Udon Thani
- ❏ Uthai Thani
- ❏ Uttaradit
- ❏ Yala
- ❏ Yasothon

Major Cities (82)

- ❏ Amnat Charoen: Amnat Charoen
- ❏ Bueng Kan: Bueng Kan
- ❏ Buriram: Buriram
- ❏ Chai Nat: Chai Nat
- ❏ Chaiyaphum: Chaiyaphum
- ❏ Chanthaburi: Chanthaburi
- ❏ Chiang Mai: Chiang Mai
- ❏ Chiang Mai: Fang
- ❏ Chiang Mai: Omkoi
- ❏ Chiang Mai: Samoeng
- ❏ Chiang Rai: Chiang Khlong
- ❏ Chiang Rai: Chiang Rai
- ❏ Chiang Rai: Mae Chan
- ❏ Chiang Rai: Mae Sai
- ❏ Chonburi: Chonburi
- ❏ Chonburi: Pattaya
- ❏ Chonburi: Sattahip
- ❏ Chonburi: Si Racha
- ❏ Chumphon: Chumphon
- ❏ Kamphaeng Phet: Kamphaeng Phet
- ❏ Kanchanaburi: Kanchanaburi
- ❏ Khon Kaen: Khon Kaen
- ❏ Lampang: Lampang
- ❏ Lamphun: Lamphun
- ❏ Loei: Chiang Khan
- ❏ Loei: Loei
- ❏ Lopburi: Lopburi
- ❏ Mae Hong Son: Mae Hong Son
- ❏ Mae Hong Son: Pai

- Mae Hong Son: Mae Sariang
- Maha Sarakham: Maha Sarakham
- Mukdahan: Mukdahan
- Nakhon Pathom: Nakhon Pathom
- Nakhon Phanom: Nakhon Phanom
- Nakhon Ratchasima: Nakhon Ratchasima
- Nakhon Ratchasima: Pak Chong
- Nakhon Sawan: Nakhon Sawan
- Nakhon Si Thammarat: Nakhon Si Thammarat
- Nan: Bo Kluea
- Nan: Nan
- Narathiwat: Narathiwat
- Nong Bua Lamphu: Nong Bua Lamphu
- Nong Khai: Nong Khai
- Nonthaburi: Nonthaburi
- Nonthaburi: Pak Kret
- Pathum Thani: Khlong Luang
- Pattani: Pattani
- Phang Nga: Phang Nga
- Phatthalung: Phatthalung
- Phayao: Ban Mai
- Phetchabun: Phetchabun
- Phetchaburi: Phetchaburi
- Phichit: Phichit
- Phitsanulok: Phitsanulok
- Phra Nakhon Si Ayutthaya: Phra Nakhon Si Ayutthaya (also called just Ayutthaya)
- Phrae: Phrae
- Phuket: Phuket

- Prachuap Khiri Khan: Hua Hin
- Ranong: Ranong
- Ratchaburi: Ratchaburi
- Rayong: Rayong
- Roi Et: Roi Et
- Sakon Nakhon: Sakon Nakhon
- Samut Prakan: Samut Prakan
- Samut Sakhon: Samut Sakhon
- Saraburi: Saraburi
- Sisaket: Sisaket
- Songkhla: Hat Yai
- Songkhla: Songkhla
- Sukhothai: Sukhothai
- Surat Thani: Surat Thani
- Surin: Surin
- Tak: Mae Sot
- Tak: Tak
- Trang: Trang
- Trat: Trat
- Ubon Ratchathani: Ubon Ratchathani
- Udon Thani: Udon Thani
- Uttaradit: Uttaradit
- Yala: Yala
- Yasothon: Yasothon

Favorite Tourist Destinations (165)

- Amnat Charoen: Wat Pho Sila
- Amnat Charoen: Wat Saman Rattanaram
- Ang Thong: Wat Chanthraram
- Bangkok: Canals
- Bangkok: Chatuchak Weekend Market

- Bangkok: Floating Market
- Bangkok: The Grand Palace
- Bangkok: Jim Thompson House
- Bangkok: Khao San Road
- Bangkok: Lumpini Park
- Bangkok: Nana Plaza
- Bangkok: Patpong
- Bangkok: Soi Cowboy
- Bangkok: Sukhumvit Road
- Bangkok: Wat Arun (Temple of the Dawn)
- Bangkok: Wat Pho
- Bangkok: Wat Phra Gaew (Temple of the Emerald Buddha)
- Bueng Kan: Wat Ahong
- Bueng Kan: Wat Phu Tok (Stairways to Heaven)
- Buriram: Phanom Rung Historical Park
- Chachoengsao: Wat Sothorn
- Chai Nat: Wat Phra Borommathat Worawihan
- Chaiyaphum: Prang Ku
- Chanthaburi: Chanthaboon Old Town
- Chiang Mai: Chiang Mai Night Bazaar
- Chiang Mai: Mae Fah Luang Art and Cultural Park
- Chiang Mai and Chiang Rai: Northern Hill Tribes
- Chiang Mai: Queen Sirikit Botanic Garden
- Chiang Mai: Royal Park Rajapruek

- ❏ Chiang Mai: San Kamphaeng Hot Springs
- ❏ Chiang Mai: Sunday Walking Street Market
- ❏ Chiang Mai: Wat Chedi Luang
- ❏ Chiang Mai: Wat Ched Yod
- ❏ Chiang Mai: Wat Phra That Doi Kham (Temple of the Golden Mountain)
- ❏ Chiang Mai: Wat Phra That Doi Suthep (Temple of Suthep Mountain)
- ❏ Chiang Rai: Hall of Opium Museum
- ❏ Chiang Rai: Phu Chi Fah
- ❏ Chiang Rai: Wat Rong Khun (White Temple)
- ❏ Chonburi: Jomtien Beach
- ❏ Chonburi: Pattaya Floating Market
- ❏ Chonburi: Pattaya Walking Street
- ❏ Elephant Sanctuary: Any one of the many will suffice
- ❏ Kalasin: Phu Faek Forest Park
- ❏ Kalasin: Sirindhorn Museum and Phu Kum Khao Dinosaur Excavation Site
- ❏ Kamphaeng Phet: Kamphaeng Phet Historical Park
- ❏ Kanchanaburi: Bridge on the River Kwai
- ❏ Kanchanaburi: Death Railway
- ❏ Kanchanaburi: Hellfire Pass Interpretive Centre and Memorial Walking Trail
- ❏ Kanchanaburi: Prasat Mueang Sing Historical Park

- ❑ Kanchanaburi: Thailand-Burma Railway Centre
- ❑ Kanchanaburi: Three Pagodas Pass
- ❑ Khon Kaen: Si Wiang Dinosaur Park
- ❑ Khon Kaen: Wat Nong Wang
- ❑ Khon Kaen: Wat Thung Setthi
- ❑ Krabi: Ao Nang
- ❑ Krabi: Klong Thom Hot Springs
- ❑ Krabi: Rai Leh Beach
- ❑ Lampang: Baan Sao Nak
- ❑ Lampang: Dhanabadee Ceramic Museum
- ❑ Lampang: Wat Phra Kaeo Don Tao Suchadaram
- ❑ Lamphun: Wat Phra That Hariphunchai
- ❑ Lamphun: Wat San Pa Yang Luang
- ❑ Loei: Erawan Cave
- ❑ Loei: Wat Pahuaylad Temple
- ❑ Lopburi: King Narai's Palace
- ❑ Lopburi: Phra Prang Sam Yod
- ❑ Lopburi: Wat Phra Si Ratana Maha That
- ❑ Mae Hong Son: Pai Canyon
- ❑ Mae Hong Son: Pai Historical Bridge
- ❑ Mae Hong Son: Tham Lot (Fish Cave)
- ❑ Maha Sarakham: Wat Phra That Na Dun
- ❑ Mukdahan: Indochine Market
- ❑ Mukdahan: Wat Si Mongkhon Tai
- ❑ Nakhon Nayok: Bamboo Grove Wat Chulaporn Wararam

- ❏ Nakhon Pathom: Sanam Chandra Palace
- ❏ Nakhon Pathom: Wat Phra Pathom Chedi
- ❏ Nakhon Phanom: Paya Sri Satta Nakarat
- ❏ Nakhon Phanom: Wat Maha That
- ❏ Nakhon Ratchasima: Giant Banyan Tree (Sai Ngam)
- ❏ Nakhon Ratchasima: Phimai Historical Park
- ❏ Nakhon Ratchasima: Thao Suranaree Monument
- ❏ Nakhon Sawan: Wat Kiriwong
- ❏ Nakhon Si Thammarat: Wat Chedi (Chicken Temple)
- ❏ Nan: Nan Walking Street
- ❏ Nan: Wat Phra That Chae Haeng
- ❏ Nan: Wat Phra That Khao Noi
- ❏ Nan: Wat Phumin
- ❏ Narathiwat: Narathat Beach
- ❏ Narathiwat: Taloh-manoh Mosque
- ❏ Nong Bua Lamphu: Somdej Phra Naresuan Maharat Shrine
- ❏ Nong Bua Lamphu: Wat Thom Klong Pen
- ❏ Nong Khai: Sala Kaew Ku
- ❏ Nong Khai: Thai-Lao Friendship Bridge
- ❏ Nong Khai: Tha Sadet Market
- ❏ Nong Khai: Wat Pha Tak Sua
- ❏ Nonthaburi: Wat Sangkhathan

- ❏ Pathum Thani: The National Museum
- ❏ Pattani: Krue Se Mosque
- ❏ Pattani: Pattani Provincial Central Mosque
- ❏ Pattani: Wat Chang Hai Rat Buranaram
- ❏ Phang Nga: International Tsunami Museum
- ❏ Phatthalung: Khao Ok Thalu
- ❏ Phatthalung: Thale Noi Water Bird Park
- ❏ Phayao: Phu Langka Forest Park
- ❏ Phayao: Wat Analayo Thipphayaram
- ❏ Phetchabun: Wat Pha Sorn Kaew (Temple on a High Glass Cliff)
- ❏ Phetchaburi: Phra Nakhon Khiri Historical Park
- ❏ Phichit: Wat Pho Prathap Chang
- ❏ Phitsanulok: Phra Buddha Chinnarat
- ❏ Phitsanulok: Phra Si Ratana Temple
- ❏ Phra Nakhon Si Ayutthaya: Ayutthaya Historical Park
- ❏ Phra Nakhon Si Ayutthaya: Wat Chaiwatthanaram
- ❏ Phra Nakhon Si Ayutthaya: Wat Mahathat
- ❏ Phra Nakhon Si Ayutthaya: Wat Phra Sri Sanphet
- ❏ Phrae: Khum Chao Luang
- ❏ Phrae: Wat Phra That Cho Hae
- ❏ Phuket: Bangla Road
- ❏ Phuket: Bang Tao Beach

- ❏ Phuket: Big Buddha
- ❏ Phuket: Freedom Beach
- ❏ Phuket: Karon Beach
- ❏ Phuket: Phang Nga Bay
- ❏ Phuket: Promthep Cape
- ❏ Prachinburi: Prachinburi National Museum
- ❏ Prachuap Khiri Khan: Ao Manao
- ❏ Prachuap Khiri Khan: Hua Hin Beach
- ❏ Prachuap Khiri Khan: Wing 5
- ❏ Ratchaburi: Damnoen Saduak Floating Market
- ❏ Ratchaburi: Khao Ngoo (Snake) Rock Park
- ❏ Roi Et: Phalanchai Park
- ❏ Roi Et: Wat Pha Nam Yoi
- ❏ Sa Kaeo: Phrasat Khao Noi
- ❏ Sakon Nakhon: Wat Phra That Choeng Chum Worawihan Temple
- ❏ Samut Prakan: Ancient City
- ❏ Samut Prakan: Erawan Museum
- ❏ Samut Prakan: Wat Asokaram
- ❏ Samut Sakhon: Wat Ketmadi Si Wararam
- ❏ Samut Songkhram: Amphawa Floating Market
- ❏ Samut Songkhram: Maekhlong Railway Market
- ❏ Saraburi: Wat Pasawangboon

- ❏ Sing Buri: Monument of Bang Rachan Heroes
- ❏ Sisaket: Prasat Hin Wat Sa Kampaeng Yai
- ❏ Songkhla: Tang Kuan Hill
- ❏ Sukhothai: Sukhothai Historical Park
- ❏ Suphan Buri: Wat Pa Lelai Woraviharn
- ❏ Surat Thani: Surat Thani City Pillar Shrine
- ❏ Surin: Surin National Museum
- ❏ Tak: Giant Krabak Tree
- ❏ Tak: Tee Lor Su Waterfall
- ❏ Tak: Thailand-Myanmar Friendship Bridge
- ❏ Tak: Wat Thai Wattanaram
- ❏ Ubon Ratchathani: Wat Nong Pah Pong
- ❏ Ubon Ratchathani: Wat Phra That Nong Bua
- ❏ Udon Thani: National Museum of Ban Chiang
- ❏ Udon Thani: Nong Prajak Public Park
- ❏ Udon Thani: Phu Phrabat Historical Park
- ❏ Uthai Thani: Giant Tree in Baan Rai
- ❏ Uthai Thani: Wat Tham Khao Wong
- ❏ Uthai Thani: Wat Tha Sung
- ❏ Uttaradit: Praya Phichai Dap Hak Memorial
- ❏ Uttaradit: Sak Yai Forest Park
- ❏ Uttaradit: Wat Phra Thaen Sila At

- ❏ Yala: Piyamit Tunnels and Millennium Tree
- ❏ Yala: Talay Mok Aiyoeweng
- ❏ Yasothon: Phu Tham Phra

National and Marine Parks (131)

- ❏ Buriram and Sa Kaeo: Ta Phraya National Park
- ❏ Chaiyaphum: Pa Hin Ngam National Park
- ❏ Chaiyaphum: Phu Laenkha National Park
- ❏ Chaiyaphum: Sai Thong National Park
- ❏ Chaiyaphum: Tat Ton National Park
- ❏ Chanthaburi: Khao Khitchakut National Park
- ❏ Chanthaburi: Khao Sip Ha Chan National Park
- ❏ Chanthaburi: Namtok Phlio National Park
- ❏ Chiang Mai: Doi Inthanon National Park
- ❏ Chiang Mai: Doi Pha Hom Pok National Park
- ❏ Chiang Mai: Doi Suthep-Pui National Park
- ❏ Chiang Mai: Huai Nam Dang National Park
- ❏ Chiang Mai: Khun Khan National Park
- ❏ Chiang Mai: Mae Wang National Park
- ❏ Chiang Mai: Op Luang National Park
- ❏ Chiang Mai: Pha Daeng National Park
- ❏ Chiang Mai: Si Lanna National Park

- Chiang Rai, Lampang, and Phayao: Doi Luang National Park
- Chiang Rai: Khun Chae National Park
- Chumphon: Mu Koh Chumphon National Marine Park
- Kamphaeng Phet: Khlong Lan National Park
- Kamphaeng Phet and Tak: Khlong Wang Chao National Park
- Kamphaeng Phet and Nakhon Sawan: Mae Wong National Park
- Kanchanaburi: Chaloem Rattanakosin National Park
- Kanchanaburi: Erawan National Park
- Kanchanaburi: Khao Laem National Park
- Kanchanaburi: Khuean Srinagarindra National Park
- Kanchanaburi: Lam Khlong Ngu National Park
- Kanchanaburi: Sai Yok National Park
- Kanchanaburi: Thong Pha Phum National Park
- Khon Kaen and Chaiyaphum: Nam Phong National Park
- Khon Kaen: Phu Kao-Phu Phan Kham National Park
- Khon Kaen and Loei: Phu Pha Man National Park
- Khon Kaen: Phu Wiang National Park
- Krabi: Hat Noppharat Thara-Mu Koh Phi Phi National Marine Park

- ❑ Krabi: Khao Phanom Bencha National Marine Park
- ❑ Krabi: Mu Koh Lanta National Marine Park
- ❑ Krabi: Than Bok Khorani National Park
- ❑ Lampang: Chae Son National Park
- ❑ Lampang and Tak: Mae Wa National Park
- ❑ Lamphun: Doi Khun Tan National Park
- ❑ Lamphun, Chiang Mai, and Tak: Mae Ping National Park
- ❑ Loei: Phu Kradueng National Park
- ❑ Loei: Phu Ruea National Park
- ❑ Loei: Phu Suan Sai National Park
- ❑ Mae Hong Son: Namtok Mae Surin National Park
- ❑ Mae Hong Son: Salawin National Park
- ❑ Mae Hong Son: Tham Pla-Namtok Pha Suea National Park
- ❑ Mukdahan: Phu Pha Thoep National Park
- ❑ Mukdahan, Ubon Ratchathani, and Yasothon: Phu Sa Dok Bua National Park
- ❑ Nakhon Phanom: Phu Langka National Park
- ❑ Nakhon Ratchasima, Nakhon Nayok, Prachinburi, and Saraburi: Khao Yai National Park
- ❑ Nakhon Si Thammarat: Khao Luang National Park
- ❑ Nakhon Si Thammarat: Khao Nan National Park

- ❏ Nakhon Si Thammarat and Surat Thani: Namtok Si Khit National Park
- ❏ Nakhon Si Thammarat: Namtok Yong National Park
- ❏ Nan: Doi Phu Kha National Park
- ❏ Nan: Khun Nan National Park
- ❏ Nan: Mae Charim National Park
- ❏ Nan: Si Nan National Park
- ❏ Narathiwat, Pattani, and Yala: Budo-Su-Ngai Padi National Park
- ❏ Pattani, Songkhla, and Yala: Namtok Sai Khao National Park
- ❏ Phang Nga: Ao Phang-Nga National Marine Park
- ❏ Phang Nga: Khao Lak-Lam Ru National Marine Park
- ❏ Phang Nga: Khao Lampi-Hat Thai Mueang National Marine Park
- ❏ Phang Nga: Mu Koh Similan National Marine Park
- ❏ Phang Nga: Mu Koh Surin National Marine Park
- ❏ Phang Nga: Si Phang-Nga National Park
- ❏ Phatthalung: Khao Pu-Khao Ya National Park
- ❏ Phayao: Doi Phu Nang National Park
- ❏ Phayao and Chiang Rai: Mae Puem National Park
- ❏ Phayao and Chiang Rai: Phu Sang National Park
- ❏ Phetchabun: Khao Kho National Park
- ❏ Phetchabun: Nam Nao National Park

- Phetchabun: Tat Mok National Park
- Phetchaburi and Prachuap Khiri Khan: Kaeng Krachan National Park
- Phitsanulok: Kaeng Chet Khwae National Park
- Phitsanulok: Namtok Chat Trakan National Park
- Phitsanulok and Loei: Phu Hin Rong Kla National Park
- Phitsanulok and Phetchabun: Thung Salaeng Luang National Park
- Phrae: Doi Pha Klong National Park
- Phrae: Mae Yom National Park
- Phrae and Lampang: Wiang Kosai National Park
- Phuket: Sirinat National Marine Park
- Prachinburi and Nakhon Ratchasima: Thap Lan National Park
- Prachuap Khiri Khan: Hat Wanakon National Marine Park
- Prachuap Khiri Khan: Khao Sam Roi Yot National Marine Park
- Prachuap Khiri Khan: Kui Buri National Park
- Prachuap Khiri Khan: Namtok Huai Yang National Park
- Ranong: Laem Son National Marine Park
- Ranong: Lam Nam Kra Buri National Marine Park
- Ranong: Mu Koh Ranong National Marine Park
- Ranong and Chumphon: Namtok Ngao National Park

- Ratchaburi: Chaloem Phrakiat Thai Prachan National Park
- Rayong and Chanthaburi: Khao Chamao-Khao Wong National Park
- Rayong: Khao Laem Ya-Mu Koh Samet National Marine Park
- Sa Kaeo and Prachinburi: Pang Sida National Park
- Sakon Nakhon and Udon Thani: Phu Pha Lek National Park
- Sakon Nakhon and Kalasin: Phu Phan National Park
- Sakon Nakhon, Mukdahan, and Nakhon Phanom: Phu Pha Yon National Park
- Saraburi: Namtok Sam Lan National Park
- Satun and Trang: Mu Koh Phetra National Marine Park
- Satun: Tarutao National Marine Park
- Satun: Thale Ban National Marine Park
- Sisaket and Ubon Ratchathani: Khao Phra Wihan National Park
- Songkhla: Khao Nam Khang National Park
- Sukhothai: Ramkhamhaeng National Park
- Sukhothai: Si Satchanalai National Park
- Suphan Buri: Phu Toei National Park
- Surat Thani: Kaeng Krung National Park

- Surat Thani: Khao Sok National Park
- Surat Thani: Khlong Phanom National Park
- Surat Thani: Mu Koh Ang Thong National Marine Park
- Surat Thani: Tai Rom Yen National Park
- Surat Thani: Than Sadet-Koh Pha-Ngan National Park
- Tak: Khun Phawo National Park
- Tak: Lan Sang National Park
- Tak: Mae Moei National Park
- Tak: Namtok Pha Charoen National Park
- Tak: Taksin Maharat National Park
- Trang: Hat Chao Mai National Marine Park
- Trat: Mu Koh Chang National Marine Park
- Trat: Namtok Khlong Kaeo National Park
- Ubon Ratchathani: Kaeng Tana National Park
- Ubon Ratchathani: Pha Taem National Park
- Ubon Ratchathani: Phu Chong-Na Yoi National Park
- Udon Thani: Na Yung-Nam Som National Park
- Uttaradit and Phrae: Lam Nam Nan National Park
- Uttaradit: Phu Soi Dao National Park
- Uttaradit: Ton Sak Yai National Park
- Yala: Bang Lang National Park

Islands (29)

- ❏ Chonburi: Koh Sichang
- ❏ Krabi: Koh Kai (Chicken Island)
- ❏ Krabi: Koh Lanta Yai
- ❏ Krabi: Koh Phi Phi
- ❏ Phang Nga: James Bond Island (Koh Khao Phing Kan and Koh Tapu)
- ❏ Phang Nga: Koh Klang
- ❏ Phang Nga: Koh Panyi
- ❏ Phang Nga: Koh Ri
- ❏ Phang Nga: Koh Surin Tai
- ❏ Phang Nga: Koh Tapu
- ❏ Phang Nga: Koh Yao Yai
- ❏ Ranong: Koh Phayam
- ❏ Rayong: Koh Samet
- ❏ Satun: Koh Adang
- ❏ Satun: Koh Lipe
- ❏ Satun: Koh Tarutao
- ❏ Surat Thani: Koh Nang Yuan
- ❏ Surat Thani: Koh Phaluai
- ❏ Surat Thani: Koh Pha Ngan
- ❏ Surat Thani: Koh Samui
- ❏ Surat Thani: Koh Tao
- ❏ Trat: Koh Chang
- ❏ Trat: Koh Kut
- ❏ Trat: Koh Mak
- ❏ Trat: Koh Rang
- ❏ Trang: Koh Kradan
- ❏ Trang: Koh Libong
- ❏ Trang: Koh Muk
- ❏ Trang: Koh Sukon

Rivers (34)

- ❏ Bang Pakong River (Chachoengsao and Prachinburi)
- ❏ Chanthaburi River (Chanthaburi)
- ❏ Chao Praya River (Ang Thong, Bangkok, Chainat, Nakhon Sawan, and Phra Nakhon Si Ayutthaya, Nonthaburi, Pathum Thani, Samut Prakan, Sing Buri, and Uthai Thani)
- ❏ Chi River (Chaiyaphum, Kalasin, Khon Kaen, Maha Sarakham, Nakhon Ratchasima, Roi Et, Yasothon, and Ubon Ratchathani)
- ❏ Hueang River (Loei)
- ❏ Ing River (Chiang Rai and Phayao)
- ❏ Khwae Yai River (Kanchanaburi and Tak)
- ❏ Kok River (Chiang Mai and Chiang Rai)
- ❏ Li River (Chiang Mai and Lamphun)
- ❏ Loei River (Loei and Phetchabun)
- ❏ Lopburi River (Phra Nakhon Si Ayutthaya, and Saraburi)
- ❏ Mae Khlong River (Kanchanaburi, Ratchaburi, and Samut Songkhram)
- ❏ Mae Sai River (Chiang Rai)
- Mekong River (Amnat Charoen, Bueng Kan, Chiang Rai, Loei, Mukdahan, Nakhon Phahom, Nong Khai, and Ubon Ratchathani)

(checkable under extreme points)
- Moei River (Mae Hong Son)
- Mun River (Buriram, Nakhon Ratchasima, Sisaket, Surin, and Ubon Ratchathani)
- Nakon Nayok River (Nakon Nayok and Prachinburi)
- Nan River (Nakhon Sawan, Nan, Phichit, Phitsanulok, and Uttaradit)
- Noi River (Chainat, Phra Nakhon Si Ayutthaya, and Singburi)
- Pak Phanang River (Nakhon Si Thammarat)
- Pai River (Mae Hong Son)
- Pa Sak River (Loei, Lopburi, Phetchabun, Phra Nakhon Si Ayutthaya, and Saraburi)
- Pattani River (Pattani and Yala)
- Phachi River (Kanchanaburi and Ratchaburi)
- Phetchaburi River (Phetchaburi)
- Ping River (Chiang Mai, Kamphaeng Phet, Lamphun, Nakhon Sawan, and Tak)
- Ruak River (Chiang Rai)
- Sakae Krang River (Chainat, Kamphaeng Phet, and Nakhon Sawan)
- Salween River (Mae Hong Son)
- Tapi River (Nakhon Si Thammarat)
- Tha Chin River (Chainat, Nakhon Pathom, Samut Sakhon, and Suphan Buri)

- ❏ Trang River (Nakhon Si Thammarat and Trang)
- ❏ Wang River (Chiang Rai, Lampang, and Tak)
- ❏ Wa River (Nan)
- ❏ Yom River (Nakhon Sawan, Phayao, Phichit, Phitsanulok, Phrae, and Sukhothai)

Dams, Reservoirs, and Lakes (44)

- ❏ Chai Nat: Chao Phraya Dam
- ❏ Chaiyaphum: Chulabhorn Dam
- ❏ Chaiyaphum: Huai Kum Dam
- ❏ Chiang Mai: Huay Tung Tao Dam
- ❏ Chiang Mai: Mae Ngat Somboon Chon Dam
- ❏ Kalasin: Lam Pao Dam
- ❏ Kanchanaburi: Srinagarind Dam
- ❏ Kanchanaburi: Tha Thung Na Dam
- ❏ Kanchanaburi: Vajiralongkorn Dam
- ❏ Khon Kaen: Ubol Ratana Dam
- ❏ Loei: Hua Krathing Reservoir
- ❏ Lopburi: Pa Sak Jolasid Dam
- ❏ Lopburi: Sub Lek Reservoir
- ❏ Mae Hong Son: Pang Ung Lake
- ❏ Maha Sarakham: Khae Loeng Chan Reservoir
- ❏ Maha Sarakham: Mai Kae Dam
- ❏ Nakhon Nayok: Khun Dan Prakan Chon Dam

- Nakhon Ratchasima: Lam Phra Phloeng Dam
- Nakhon Ratchasima: Lam Takhong Dam
- Nakhon Sawan: Bueng Boraphet
- Nakhon Sawan: Mae Wong Dam
- Nakhon Si Thammarat: Khao Phlai Dam
- Phayao: Phayao Lake
- Phetchaburi: Kaeng Krachan Dam
- Phichit: Bueng Si Fai
- Phitsanulok: Kwae Noi Bamrung Daen Dam
- Phuket: Bang Wad Reservoir
- Phrae: Kaeng Suea Ten Dam
- Prachinburi: Naruebodindrachinta Reservoir
- Prachuap Khiri Khan: Pranburi Dam
- Sakon Nakhon: Nam Pung Dam
- Sakon Nakhon: Nam Un Dam
- Sakon Nakhon: Nong Han Lake
- Sisaket: Hua Na Dam
- Sisaket: Rasi Salai Dam
- Songkhla and Phatthalung: Songkhla Lake (lagoon that has an outlet to the sea)
- Sukhothai: Saritphong Dam
- Suphan Buri: Krasiao Dam
- Surat Thani: Cheow Lan Lake (or Rajjaprabha Dam Reservoir)

Tak: Bhumibol Dam (checkable under extreme points)

- ❏ Ubon Ratchathani: Pak Mun Dam
- ❏ Ubon Ratchathani: Sirindhorn Dam
- ❏ Udon Thani: Nong Han Kumphawapi Lake (Red Lotus Lake)
- ❏ Uttaradit: Sirikit Dam
- ❏ Yala: Bang Lang Dam

Extreme Points (9)

- ❏ Highest Mountain Summit: 2,565 meters, Doi Inthanon, Chiang Mai
- ❏ Longest River flowing through Thailand: 4,350 kilometers, Mekong River (Amnat Charoen, Bueng Kan, Chiang Rai, Loei, Mukdahan, Nakhon Phahom, Nong Khai, Ubon Ratchathani)
- Longest River flowing entirely in Thailand: Some sources say the Chi River is 765 kilometers long and others say it's 1,047 kilometers long; the Mun River is listed as 900 kilometers long. Both rivers are checkable in the rivers chapter.
- ❏ Tallest Building: 314 meters, King Power Mahanakhon, Bangkok
- ❏ Highest Dam: 154 meters, Bhumibol Dam, Tak
- Highest Temperature Ever Recorded: 44.6° C, Mae Hong Son,

Mae Hong Son (included elsewhere) Lowest Temperature Ever Recorded: in 1974 −1.4° C, Sakhon Nakhon, Sakhon Nakhon, but may have been lowered recently to −5.0° C at Doi Inthanon Summit, Chiang Mai (included elsewhere)
❑ Biggest Tree in Circumference: 24.2 meters in girth, Koh Yao Noi, Phang Nga
❑ Eastern-Most Point: Pha Taem, Ubon Ratchathani, Laotian border
❑ Western-Most Point: Mae Nam Salawin in Mae Sam Laep, Mae Hong Son, Myanmar border
❑ Northern-Most Point: Mae Sai, Chiang Rai, Myanmar border
❑ Southern-Most Point: Betong, Yala, Malaysian border

Mountains (9)

Doi Inthanon: 2,565 meters, Chiang Mai (checkable under extreme points)
❑ Doi Pha Hom Pok: Chiang Mai, 2,296 meters
❑ Doi Chiang Dao: Chiang Mai, 2,175 meters
❑ Khao Kacheu Lau: Tak, 2,152 meters
❑ Phu Soi Dao: Uttaradit, 2,120 meters

- ❏ Phu Khe: Nan, 2,079 meters
- ❏ Phu Lo: Nan, 2,077 meters
- ❏ Doi Mae Tho: Chiang Rai, 2,031 meters
- ❏ Doi Mae Ya: Mae Hong Son, 2,005 meters
- ❏ Doi Phong Sa Yan: Mae Hong Son, 2,004 meters

Scuba Diving Sites (50)

- ❏ Anemone Reef
- ❏ Anita's Reef (Tsunami Memorial)
- ❏ Aow Leuk
- ❏ Boonsung Wreck
- ❏ Boulder City
- ❏ Bremen Wreck
- ❏ Christmas Point
- ❏ Chumphon Pinnacle
- ❏ East of Eden
- ❏ Elephant Head Rock (Hin Pusar)
- ❏ Hardeep Wreck
- ❏ Hin Bida
- ❏ Hin Daeng
- ❏ Hin Ga Daeng
- ❏ Hin Kuak Ma
- ❏ Hin Luk Bat
- ❏ Hin Muang
- ❏ Hin Pae
- ❏ Hin Rap
- ❏ HTMS Chang
- ❏ HTMS Khram
- ❏ HTMS Kut
- ❏ HTMS Mataphon
- ❏ HTMS Sattakut
- ❏ Japanese Garden
- ❏ King Cruiser Wreck
- ❏ Koh Bangu
- ❏ Koh Bida Nai
- ❏ Koh Bida Nok
- ❏ Koh Bon
- ❏ Koh Chi
- ❏ Koh Dok Mai
- ❏ Koh Haa
- ❏ Koh Khai

- ❏ Koh Khrok
- ❏ Koh Larn
- ❏ Koh Nang Yuan
- ❏ Koh Phi Phi
- ❏ Koh Sak
- ❏ Koh Tachai
- ❏ Racha Noi
- ❏ Racha Yai
- ❏ Richelieu Rock
- ❏ Sail Rock
- ❏ Shark Fin Reef
- ❏ Shark Point (Hin Musang)
- ❏ Southern Rock
- ❏ Stonehenge (Similan)
- ❏ Twin Peaks
- ❏ West of Eden

Notes:

www.ingramcontent.com/pod-product-compliance
Lightning Source LLC
LaVergne TN
LVHW091307080426
835510LV00007B/399